Scotland's leading educational publishers

D1323348

Practice Papers for SQA Exams

Intermediate 2

English

Published by
Leckie & Leckie Ltd
An imprint of HarperCollins*Publishers*
Westerhill Road, Bishopbriggs, Glasgow G64 2QT
T: 0844 576 8126 F: 0844 576 8131
leckieandleckie@harpercollins.co.uk   www.leckieandleckie.co.uk

Special thanks to
Exemplarr (layout and illustration),
Jill Laidlaw (copy-edit),
Felicity Kendall (proofread),
Helen Bleck (proofread)

A CIP Catalogue record for this book is available from the British Library.

® Leckie & Leckie is a registered trademark.

Leckie & Leckie is grateful to the following companies for permission to reproduce their material:

Extract from *Ever By My Side: A Memoir in Eight (Acts) Pets*, reprinted by permission of Broadway Books, an imprint of The Crown Publishing Group © Nick Trout (Close Reading Exam A).

Extract from *Stephen Fry in America*, reprinted by permission of HarperCollins Publishers © Stephen Fry (Close Reading exam B).

Extract from *Buy, Buy Baby*, reprinted by permission of HarperCollins Publishers © Susan Gregory Thomas (Close Reading exam C).

Extract from *Dry Storeroom No. 1: The Secret Life of the Natural History Museum*, reprinted by permission of HarperCollins Publishers © Richard Fortey (Close Reading exam D).

Every effort has been made to trace the copyright holders and to obtain their permission for the use of copyright material. Leckie & Leckie will gladly receive information enabling them to rectify any error or omission in subsequent editions.

Questions and answers in this book do not emanate from SQA. All of our entirely new and original Practice Papers have been written by experienced authors working directly for the publisher.

Introduction

Layout of the book

This book contains brand new practice exam papers, which mirror the actual SQA exam as much as possible. The layout, paper colour and question level are all similar to the actual exam that you will sit, so that you are familiar with what the exam paper will look like.

The answer section is at the back of the book. Each answer contains a worked out answer so that you can see how the right answer has been arrived at. The answers also include practical tips on how to tackle certain types of questions, details of how marks are awarded and advice on just what the examiners will be looking for.

As the name suggests, this book is a volume of **More** Practice Exam Papers for Intermediate 2 English. Its sister publication (ISBN: 978-1-84372-777-4 Intermediate 2 English Practice Papers for SQA Exams) is also available and packed full of entirely different practice exams, worked answers and helpful explanations, hints and exam tips.

How to use this book

The Practice Papers can be used in two main ways:

1. You can complete an entire practice paper as preparation for the final exam. If you would like to use the book in this way, you can either complete the practice paper under exam-style conditions, by setting yourself a time for each paper and answering it as well as possible (without using any references or notes). Alternatively, you can answer the practice paper questions as a revision exercise (using your notes to produce a model answer). Your teacher may mark these for you.

2. You can use the Index of Question Types at the front of this book to find all the questions within the book that deal with a specific topic. This allows you to focus specifically on areas that you particularly want to revise.

Revision advice

Work out a revision timetable for each week's work in advance – remember to cover all of your subjects and to leave time for homework and breaks. For example:

Day	6pm–6.45pm	7pm–8pm	8.15pm–9pm	9.15pm–10pm
Monday	Homework	Homework	English revision	Chemistry Revision
Tuesday	Maths Revision	Physics revision	Homework	Free
Wednesday	Geography Revision	Modern Studies Revision	English Revision	French Revision
Thursday	Homework	Maths Revision	Chemistry Revision	Free
Friday	Geography Revision	French Revision	Free	Free
Saturday	Free	Free	Free	Free
Sunday	Modern Studies Revision	Maths Revision	Modern Studies Revision	Homework

Make sure that you have at least one evening free a week to relax, socialise and re-charge your batteries. It also gives your brain a chance to process the information that you have been feeding it all week.

Arrange your study time into one hour or 30 minute sessions, with a break between sessions, e.g. 6pm–7pm, 7.15pm–7.45pm, 8pm–9pm. Try to start studying as early as possible in the evening when your brain is still alert.

Study a different subject in each session, except for the day before an exam.

Do something different during your breaks between study sessions – have a cup of tea, or listen to some music.

Have your class notes and any textbooks available for your revision to hand as well as plenty of blank paper, a pen, etc. You may like to make keyword sheets like the example below:

Keyword	Meaning
Tone	The way somebody says or writes something as an indicator of what that person is feeling or thinking.
Theme	Topic or recurring idea in a piece of writing.
Plot	The story or sequence of events in a novel, play or film.

Finally, forget or ignore all or some of the advice in this section if you are happy with your present way of studying. Everyone revises differently, so find a way that works for you!

Transfer your knowledge

As well as using your class notes and textbooks to revise, these practice papers will also be a useful revision tool as they will help you to get used to answering exam-style questions. The 'Worked Answers' section at the back of the book will show you how to read and interpret Close Reading questions so that you answer them clearly and correctly and, in the Critical Essay questions section, how to apply your knowledge of the text or topic to answer the question.

Command words

In the practice papers and in the exam itself, a number of command words are used in the questions. These command words show how you should answer a question – some words indicate that you should write more than others. If you familiarise yourself with these command words, it will help you to structure your answers more effectively.

Command Word	Meaning/Explanation
Identify	Used in Close Reading – it asks you to find something, often a technique used by the writer. Sometimes you have to name the technique; at other times find an example of the technique being used.
Suggest	Used in Close Reading. Give more than just simple information – perhaps a reason or an idea.
Show	A word used in Close Reading and Critical Essay questions. It means demonstrate by analysis.
Describe	Used in Close Reading. Give more detail than you would in a basic outline, and use examples where you can.
Explain	Used in Close Reading. Discuss why an action has been taken or an outcome reached or a word/technique chosen – what are the reasons and/or processes behind it.
Justify	Used in Close Reading. Give reasons for your answer, stating why you have reached a particular conclusion.
Define	Used in Close Reading. Give the meaning of the term.
Compare	Used in Close Reading. Give the key features of two different items or ideas and discuss their similarities and/or their differences.

In the exam

Watch your time and pace yourself carefully. Work out roughly how much time you can spend on each answer and try to stick to this. For example, don't spend more than 45 minutes on each essay in the Critical Essay paper.

Be clear before the exam what the instructions are likely to be, e.g. how many questions you should answer in each section. The practice papers will help you to become familiar with the exam's instructions.

Read the question thoroughly before you begin to answer it – make sure you know exactly what the question is asking you to do. If the question is in sections (e.g. 2(a), 2(b), etc.) make sure that you answer all sections.

For the Critical Essay paper, plan your answer by jotting down keywords, key quotes or references, a mindmap or reminders of the important things to include in your answer.

Don't repeat yourself as you will not get any more marks for saying the same thing twice.

Give proper explanations. A common error is to give descriptions rather than explanations. If you are asked to explain something, you should be giving reasons. Check your answer to an 'explain' question and make sure that you have used plenty of linking words and phrases such as 'because', 'this means that', 'therefore', 'so that', 'due to', 'since' and 'the reason is'.

More English Intermediate 2 Practice Papers

This book contains four complete Intermediate 2 English exam papers. The questions featured in both the Close Reading and the Critical Essay sections are the kind of questions that come up every year in the SQA exam. Using this book will help you to become familiar with exam questions. As mentioned above, you could either work through the materials as complete exam papers, or use them to help you revise particular questions. The answer section at the end of the book is designed not just to give you the answers, but, more importantly, to explain the answers, and to give you some help with how to arrive at the answers. In the Critical Essay section of the answers we have tried to give you some guidance about how to approach the questions, and an idea of how to plan your answers. We have mentioned a few texts which you may have studied, but only to help explain a point – there are no set texts in Intermediate 2 English. Prepare for the exam with the texts you have studied and those you enjoyed.

The four papers can be tackled in any order, but we have made the first Close Reading paper ('Ever By My Side') an easier read than the other three. If you are working through the book yourself, or are using the book early in the course, it would be a good idea to start with this one. Close Reading is just as it says: a test of your ability to read a text closely and carefully. It tests your understanding of a text and your ability to analyse what the writer is trying to do; it also asks you to evaluate the writing. Remember, the best way to prepare yourself is to read, and think about what you are read, not just do practice papers like these. Even if you don't especially enjoy reading novels or long texts, you can improve your reading skills by reading newspapers or magazines. Start by reading what interests you: several newspapers contain high-quality sports sections, or have extended interviews with actors, musicians or prominent people in the weekend magazines.

Before your exam it would be a good idea to skim through all of the Critical Essay papers, just to make sure you can answer two questions from each paper. The questions are not designed to catch you out, rather to give you the opportunity to write about the texts you have studied throughout the year.

Good luck!

Indices of Question Types

In Close Reading, there are three main question types:
- Understanding – questions which ask you to explain your understanding of the ideas and details in the passage – *what* the writer has said.
- Analysis – questions which ask you to identify the techniques the writer has used to express these ideas – *how* it has been said.
- Evaluation – questions which ask for you to comment on how effective the writer has been, using appropriate evidence from the passage – *how well* it has been said.

Table 1

Table 1 shows you the question numbers for these question types so that, for example, if you want to practise evaluation questions, you could try questions 14 in Exams B and C and questions 15 in Exams A and D.

Type of question	Exam A Close Reading	Exam B Close Reading	Exam C Close Reading	Exam D Close Reading	Knowledge for Prelim			Knowledge for SQA Exam		
					Have difficulty	Still needs work	OK	Have difficulty	Still needs work	OK
Understanding	1, 2, 5, 7, 10, 12, 13	1, 3, 4, 5, 7a, 7b, 8, 10, 11	1, 2, 4, 5, 7, 11, 13	1, 3, 5, 6, 8, 9, 10, 12						
Analysis	3, 4, 6, 8, 9, 11, 14	2, 6, 9, 12, 13	3, 6, 8, 9, 10, 12	2, 4, 7, 11, 13, 14						
Evaluation	15	14	14	15						

Table 2

Table 2 gives you more detail about the Analysis questions in the Practice Papers. Analysis questions are more likely to ask you about punctuation, function, word choice, imagery, sentence structure and tone. So, for example, if you want to practise answering punctuation questions, try question 10 in Exam C and question 13 in Exam D in the Close Reading Paper.

Type of question	Exam A Close Reading	Exam B Close Reading	Exam C Close Reading	Exam D Close Reading	Knowledge for Prelim			Knowledge for SQA Exam		
					Have difficulty	Still needs work	OK	Have difficulty	Still needs work	OK
Punctuation			10	13						
Function	8	13	8	7						
Word choice	4, 6, 9, 14	2	3, 6, 12	4, 14						
Imagery		12	9	2						
Sentence structure	3, 14	6	12							
Tone	11	9		11						

Table 3

Table 3 shows you the question numbers for each of the topics you are most likely to be asked about in the Critical Essay questions so that, for example, if you want to practise writing about conflict, you could try question 6 in Exam A, question 1 in Exam B or question 3 in Exam C.

Type of question	Exam A Critical Essay	Exam B Critical Essay	Exam C Critical Essay	Exam D Critical Essay	Knowledge for Prelim			Knowledge for SQA Exam		
					Have difficulty	Still needs work	OK	Have difficulty	Still needs work	OK
Character	1, 6	1, 4, 10	1, 4, 6, 12	1, 12						
Opening, Turning point, Ending	2	2, 5, 11	2, 11	3						
Issue	3, 10, 11	3	5, 7, 10	2, 4, 5						
Conflict	6	1	3							
Experience	7, 9, 12	6, 7, 8	8, 9	11						

Practice Exam A

Practice Paper A: Intermediate 2 English

Practice Papers
For SQA Exams

ENGLISH
INTERMEDIATE 2

**Exam A
Close Reading**

Answer all of the questions.

You have 1 hour to complete this paper.

Read the following passage and then answer the questions. Remember to use your own words as much as possible.

The questions ask you to demonstrate that you:

understand the ideas and details in the passage – **what the writer has said**
(**U**: Understanding)

can identify the techniques the writer has used to express these ideas – **how it has been said**
(**A**: Analysis)

can comment on how effective the writer has been, using appropriate evidence from the passage – **how well it has been said**
(**E**: Evaluation)

The code letters (U, A, E) are next to each question to make sure you know the question's purpose. The number of marks per question will give you a good idea as to how long your answer should be.

Scotland's leading educational publishers

EVER BY MY SIDE

In this autobiographical passage, Nick Trout describes an incident that took place on a family holiday in Wales.

Time has a knack for distortion – fogging the images from the past, making everything feel bigger than it really was, messing with the collage of mental snapshots pinned to the corkboard of our memory. So I have to believe the clarity with which I still see what took place on an empty beach pounded by an angry Irish Sea as a reflection of
5   its enduring influence on me.

On this particular day trip our normal family dynamic was upset by the addition of my grandma and more important, and to my dismay, her four-legged escort, the infamous and menacing Marty. Quite why we had to take the poodle with us on a car ride to a sleepy seaside town in northern Wales I will never know. All the while Marty
10   kept vigil, staring me down, defending his personal space, offering me the occasional snarl and wrinkle of his upper lip, feigning innocence and doe-eyed stares every time I complained to Grandma. There's a reason why I have always found poodles to be one of the smartest breeds of dog.

When we got there we had a picnic on the beach, adults sipping hot tea from a thermos
15   in plastic cups and commenting on the gritty sandwiches they had prepared, the ominous-looking clouds, and the threat of rain. There was the promise of ice cream later, but first my father had agreed to help Fiona build a sand castle. For some reason I was more interested in beachcombing, so my mum, Grandma, Marty, and I set off on a walk down to the water's edge.

20   This was autumn, off-season, chilly, and there were very few people out and about. The overcast sky blended into the ocean. We were wrapped up in sweaters and overcoats and the tide was way off in the distance, forcing us to head out across wet sandy flats if we wanted to get near the waves and the possibility of washed-up shells. Marty was off leash, having the time of his life, scampering around, quick and dainty,
25   hopping from one tidal pool to the next. He didn't even mind that I was holding Grandma's hand. At the water's edge it all happened so fast. The tide was still headed out, the surf crashing hard, frothy grey breakers with quite a pull washing over the sand. This was not swimming weather (in this part of Britain it rarely ever was). This was not even paddling weather, the water icy cold to the touch. So you can imagine
30   our concern when one minute Marty was gaily dancing in and out of the lapping foam and the next he was gone, disappearing out to sea, swallowed by a wall of grey water, quickly ten, fifteen yards out and drifting still further away. He didn't bark – he probably couldn't from the cold shock stealing his breath – he just tried to paddle, head up, neck outstretched, looking in my direction.

35   There are several possibilities as to how this pivotal moment in my early life might have played out. For starters, I couldn't swim, so a selfless, heroic act in which I rescued a drowning dog as motivation for a career helping animals in need was never in the cards. Besides, I'm pretty sure my mother had not packed my inflatable rubber ring.

40   At this point you would be forgiven for gasping in horror if you feared the possibility that I was some sort of malicious Damien child, a furtive witness to poor Marty's exit, seizing the opportunity to be rid of my nemesis and rival for Grandma's attention by

squandering precious time pointing out a particularly fascinating variety of seaweed before offering an inquisitive but nonchalant "So, where's Marty?"

45 Don't worry, what really happened struck me as far more impressive and has nothing to do with guilt or the quest for redemption. Seeing Marty bobbing helplessly in the waves my grandma jumped into the roiling waters and began swimming out to sea. Bear in mind, to my way of thinking, my grandma was at least two hundred years old and could hardly walk, let alone swim. She was fully clothed, not bothering to

50 remove her coat or sweater or shoes. She just dove in like she was all lubed up for a Channel crossing and headed for the little white drowning rat bobbing up and down on her horizon.

For what seemed like forever, the angry waves mocked Grandma's rescue bid, pushing her toward Marty only to pull them apart at the last moment, until finally she had

55 him in her arms, swimming back to shore and clambering back up the beach on all fours, Marty released into the shallows, able to break free, trot off, and shake himself down.

"What were you thinking?" my mum screamed, helping Grandma to her feet, taking off her own coat and putting it around her mother's shoulders. That classic cocktail

60 of anger driven by fear had gotten the better of her. "You could have got yourself killed! And for a dog!" Grandma was shaking all over, her false teeth acting just like those wind-up false teeth, chattering uncontrollably. We began walking back up the beach, back to the car, Marty staying right by her side, and I asked, "You okay, Grandma?" She looked down at me and smiled one of the coy, conspiratorial smiles

65 that she occasionally let me see, as though she knew she had been a naughty girl, but it had been worth it.

And right then it hit me that my grandma had actually put her life on the line for a creature sent by the devil to instill fear in children.

What strange spell had this toy poodle cast over my grandmother? What has stayed

70 with me, all these years later, is my incredulity over an unthinkable rescue followed by a realization that something mysterious and powerful was at work between my grandma and Marty. Trudging through the wet sand, watching a mother and daughter together, their roles reversed, and a pathetic little dog, frightened of straying and consequently getting underfoot, I was forced to concede that Grandma must really

75 love her poodle.

From *Ever by My Side* by Dr Nick Trout

QUESTIONS

1. Look again at lines 1 to 3.

   Explain **in your own words** what the writer thinks time does to our memories.
   Quote to support your answer.   2U

2. Look again at lines 3 to 5.

   In your own words explain why the writer remembers what took place at the beach so clearly. 2U

3. Look again at lines 6 to 9.

   Comment on the effectiveness of the **sentence structure** in 'Quite why we had to take the poodle with us on a car ride to a sleepy seaside town in northern Wales I will never know.' 2A

4. Look again at lines 9 to 12.

   How does the writer's **word choice** convey how the poodle behaves towards the *writer* **OR** how it behaves towards *Grandma*? 2A

5. Look again at lines 14 to 19.

   What is the meaning of 'ominous-looking' and how does the context help you to work this out? 2U

6. Look again at lines 20 to 26.

   Anthropomorphism is a technique writers use to describe an animal as though it is a human. Quote **two** examples of anthropomorphism from this paragraph. 2A

7. Look again at lines 26 to 29.

   Write down any **two** words or phrases which convey the dangerous nature of the sea **before** Marty disappears. 2U

8. Look again at lines 35 to 39.

   Explain the **function** of the first sentence in this paragraph. 2A

9. Look again at lines 35 to 39.

   How does the writer use **word choice** to create **humour** in the lines 'For starters, I couldn't swim, so a selfless, heroic act in which I rescued a drowning dog as motivation for a career helping animals in need was never in the cards. Besides, I'm pretty sure my mother had not packed my inflatable rubber ring.' **Quote** to support your answer. 2A

10. Look again at lines 40 to 44.

In your own words, explain two things the writer could have done so that Marty would not be saved. 2U

11. Look again at lines 45 to 52.

Quote an example of informal or colloquial language in this paragraph and suggest why the writer has chosen to use this type of language. 2A

12. Look again at lines 58 to 66.

In the final sentence, the writer describes his mother and grandmother as having 'their roles reversed'. **Referring only to lines 58 to 66**, explain **two** examples of this role reversal **in your own words**. 2U

13. Look again at lines 67 to 68.

Comment on how this paragraph achieves its impact. 2A

14. Look again at lines 69 to 75.

Explain **in your own words** what feelings have stayed with the writer 'all these years later'. 2U

15. Think about the passage as a whole.

To what extent do you think the writer's attitude towards Marty **changes** in this passage? Justify your answer fully. 2E

Total (30)

[End of Question Paper]

Practice Paper A: Intermediate 2 English

Practice Papers
For SQA Exams

ENGLISH
INTERMEDIATE 2

**Exam A
Critical Essay**

Answer TWO questions from this paper.

You have 1 hour 30 minutes to complete this paper.

Each question must be chosen from a different Section (A–E). You are not allowed to choose two questions from the same Section.

In all Sections you may use Scottish texts.

Write the number of each question in the margin of your answer booklet and begin each essay on a fresh page.

You should spend about 45 minutes on each essay.

The following will be assessed:

• the relevance of your essays to the questions you have chosen

• your knowledge and understanding of key elements, central concerns and significant details of the chosen texts

• your explanation of ways in which aspects of structure/style/language contribute to the meaning /effect/impact of the chosen texts

• your evaluation of the effectiveness of the chosen texts, supported by detailed and relevant evidence

• the quality and technical accuracy of your writing.

25 marks are allocated to each question. The total for this paper is 50 marks.

Scotland's leading educational publishers

SECTION A – DRAMA

> Your answer should make reference to your chosen text and to such elements as theme, structure, characterisation, plot, setting, key scene(s), conflict, climax....

1. Choose a play in which a determined woman plays a significant part.

   Explain the reasons for this determination and say how this determination affects her happiness as the play unfolds.

2. Choose a play where a relationship reaches a turning point in a key scene.

   Describe the relationship up to this point, then show the effect this turning point has on the relationship and the rest of the play.

3. Choose a play in which an issue of concern to young people is explored.

   Say what the issue is and show how the plot and characters are used to deepen your understanding of this issue.

SECTION B – PROSE

> Your answer should make reference to your chosen text and to such elements as theme, setting, key incident(s), plot, characterisation, structure, language, ideas, narrative technique, climax/turning point, description....

4. Choose a prose work (fiction or non-fiction) in which memories play a key role.

   Show how these memories affected the writer and how the writer's treatment of them made the work enjoyable or deepened your understanding of the writer's situation.

5. Choose a novel or short story that makes significant use of symbolism and/or imagery.

   Examine how the author makes use of it/them and say how it/they contributed to developing the work's theme(s) **or** to your appreciation of the text.

6. Choose a novel or short story in which a character copes with social or family or relationship difficulties.

   Describe briefly the difficulties and explain how the author aroused your sympathy for the character's situation.

SECTION C – POETRY

Your answer should make reference to your chosen text and to such elements as content, structure, theme, rhythm, word choice, sound, tone, ideas, imagery....

7. Choose a poem which describes a person's reaction to the city **or** to the natural world.

   Describe the reaction and say how the poetic techniques used helped you appreciate this reaction.

8. Choose a poem which appears to describe an everyday incident/experience but which on closer inspection is commenting more profoundly on life.

   Briefly state what the incident/experience is and go on to demonstrate how the poetic techniques employed reveal the poet's deeper comment on the human state.

9. Choose a poem written in free verse.

   Explain what poetic devices are used to shape the poet's ideas and feelings. Say how helpful you find these devices in understanding these ideas and feelings.

SECTION D – FILM AND TV DRAMA

Your answer should make reference to your chosen text and to such elements as plot, characterisation, use of camera, editing, *mise-en-scène*, setting, dialogue, music/sound effects, key sequence....

10. Choose a film or TV drama (including a single play, a serial or a series) which presents the supernatural interacting with normal everyday life.

    Briefly describe the media techniques used to make the situation believable and say how these techniques contributed to your enjoyment.

11. Choose a film or TV drama (including a single play, a serial or series) which deals with the consumer society or the world of fashion.

    Show how this society/world is explored through setting and character.

12. Choose a scene or sequence from a film or TV drama (including a single play, a serial or a series) which transports you to a setting unfamiliar to you.

    Briefly describe the setting and say which techniques helped make this setting convincing.

SECTION E – LANGUAGE

Answers to questions in this section should refer to the text and to such relevant features as register, accent, dialect, slang, jargon, vocabulary, tone, abbreviation....

13. Consider the language of news reporting in two newspapers of contrasting reporting styles.

   Say what aspects of each newspaper's language are distinctive and what advantages there are in each of their approaches.

14. Consider the language of a brochure or advertisement which you find persuasive.

   Say which persuasive techniques you noticed at work and say how effective you found them.

15. Consider the language of a group who share recreational or professional interests.

   Explain what aspects of language set them apart and what advantages their specialist language offers them.

[End of Question Paper]

Practice Exam B

Practice Paper B: Intermediate 2 English

Practice Papers
For SQA Exams

ENGLISH
INTERMEDIATE 2

Exam B
Close Reading

Answer all of the questions.

You have 1 hour to complete this paper.

Read the following passage and then answer the questions. Remember to use your own words as much as possible.

The questions ask you to demonstrate that you:

understand the ideas and details in the passage – **what the writer has said**
(**U**: Understanding)

can identify the techniques the writer has used to express these ideas – **how it has been said**
(**A**: Analysis)

can comment on how effective the writer has been, using appropriate evidence from the passage –
how well it has been said
(**E**: Evaluation)

The code letters (U, A, E) are next to each question to make sure you know the question's purpose. The number of marks per question will give you a good idea as to how long your answer should be.

Scotland's leading educational publishers

STEPHEN FRY IN AMERICA

In this opening extract from the book Stephen Fry in America, *the author explains why he wanted to make a television documentary about America.*

I was so nearly an American. It was *that* close. In the mid-50s, my father was offered a job at Princeton University. One of the reasons he turned it down was that he didn't think he liked the idea of his children growing up as Americans.

I was ten when my mother made me a present of this momentous information. The
5   very second she did so, Steve was born.

Steve looked exactly like me, same height, weight and hair colour. In fact, until we opened our mouths, it was almost impossible to distinguish one from the other. Steve's voice had the clear, penetrating, high-up-in-the-head twang of American. He called Mummy 'Mom', he used words like 'swell', 'cute' and 'darn'. There were
10   detectable differences in behaviour too. He spread jam (which he called jelly) on his (smooth, not crunchy) peanut butter sandwiches, he wore jeans, t-shirts and basketball sneakers rather than grey shorts, Aertex shirts and plimsolls. He had far more money for sweets, which he called candy, than Stephen ever did. Steve was confident almost to the point of rudeness, unlike Stephen who veered unconvincingly between shyness
15   and showing off. If I am honest, I have to confess that Stephen was slightly afraid of Steve.

Most people who are obsessed by America are fascinated by the physical – the cars, the movies, the clothes, the gadgets, the sports, the cities, the landscape and the landmarks. I am interested in all of those, of course I am, but I (perhaps because of
20   my father's decision) am interested in something more. I have always wanted to get right under the skin of American life. To know what it *really* is to be an American, to have grown up and been schooled as an American; to work and play as an American; to romance, labour, succeed, fail, feud, fight, vote, shop, drift, dream and drop out as an American; to grow old and grow ill as an American.

25   For years then, I have harboured a desire deep within me to make a documentary film about the 'real' America. Not the usual road movies in a Mustang and certainly not the kind of films where minority maniacs are trapped into making exhibitions of themselves. It is easy enough to find Americans to sneer at if you look hard enough, just as it is easy to find ludicrous and lunatic Britons to sneer at. Without the intention
30   of fawning and flattering then, I did want to make an honest film about America, an unashamed love letter to its physical beauty and a film that allowed Americans to reveal themselves in all their variety.

Anti-Americanism is said to be on the rise around the world. I have often felt a hot flare of shame inside me when I listen to my fellow Britons casually jeering at the
35   perceived depth of American ignorance, American crassness, American isolationism, American materialism, American lack of irony, American vulgarity. Aside from the sheer rudeness of such open and unapologetic mockery, it seems to me to reveal very little about America and a great deal about the rather feeble need of some Britons to feel superior. All right, they seem to be saying, we no longer have an Empire, power,
40   prestige or respect in the world, but we do have 'taste' and 'subtlety' and 'broad general knowledge', unlike those poor Yanks. What silly, self-deluding rubbish! What

small-minded stupidity! Such Britons hug themselves with the thought that they are more cosmopolitan and sophisticated than Americans because they think they know more about geography and world culture, as if *firstly* being cosmopolitan and
45 sophisticated can be scored in a quiz and as if *secondly* (and much more importantly) being cosmopolitan and sophisticated is in any way desirable or admirable to begin with. Sophistication is not a moral quality, nor is it (unless one is mad) a criterion by which one would choose one's friends. Why do we like people? Because they are knowledgeable, cosmopolitan and sophisticated? No, because they are charming,
50 kind, considerate, exciting to be with, amusing ... there is a long list, but knowing what the capital of Kazakhstan is will not be on it. Unless, as I repeat, you are mad.

The truth is, we are offended by the clear fact that so many Americans know and care so very little about us. How *dare* they not know who our Prime Minister is, or be so indifferent as to believe that Wales is an island off the coast of Scotland? We
55 are quite literally not on the map as far as they are concerned and that hurts. They can get along without us, it seems, a lot better than we can get along without them and how can that not be galling to our pride? Thus we (or some of us) react with the superiority and conceit characteristic of people who have been made to feel deeply inferior.

60 I do not believe, incidentally, that most Britons are anti-American, far from it. Many are as fascinated in a positive way by the United States as I am, and if their pride needs to be salvaged by a little affectionate banter then I suppose it does little harm.

So I wanted to make an American series which was not about how amusingly un-ironic and ignorant Americans are, nor about religious nuts and gun-toting militiamen, but
65 one which tried to penetrate everyday American life at many levels and across the whole United States.

From *Stephen Fry in America* by Stephen Fry

QUESTIONS

1. Look again at lines 1 to 5.

   Why did the author's father turn down the job at Princeton University in America? **Answer in your own words.**   2U

2. Look again at lines 4 and 5.

   Comment on the effectiveness of the writer's **word choice** in 'I was ten when my mother made me a present of this momentous information.'   2A

3. Look again at lines 4 to 16.

   In your opinion, who is Steve? Give a reason for your answer.   2U

4. Look again at line 14.

What does the expression 'veered unconvincingly' in line 14 tell you about Stephen's personality? 2U

5. Look again at lines 17 to 24.

Explain **in your own words** what Stephen wants to find out about America. Suggest a reason for this interest. 2U

6. Look again at line 21 to 24.

Comment on the effectiveness of the **sentence structure** of the sentence starting 'To know what it *really* is to ...' 2A

7. Look again at lines 25 to 32.

(*a*) **In your own words**, explain what type of film the author did NOT want to make and why. 2U

(*b*) **In your own words**, explain what type of film the author DID want to make and why. 2U

8. Look again at lines 33 to 36.

In your own words, explain why Britons make fun of Americans. 2U

9. Look again at lines 41 to 42.

How does the author establish a tone of **disapproval** in the sentences 'What silly, self-deluding rubbish! What small-minded stupidity!'? 2A

10. Look again at lines 42 to 51.

What is the meaning of 'cosmopolitan' and how does the context help you to work this out? 2U

11. Look again at lines 52 to 54.

Write down **two** words from lines 52 to 54 that show how the British feel about Americans' knowledge of Britain. 2U

12. Look again at lines 54 and 55.

Identify and explain the technique used in the phrase 'We are quite literally not on the map ...' 2A

13. Look again at lines 63 to 66.

What is the function of the word 'so' in the first sentence of the last paragraph? 2A

14. Think about the passage as a whole.

How successful has the author been in persuading you to watch his TV programme about America? Give reasons for your answer. 2E

Total (30)

[End of Question Paper]

Practice Paper B: Intermediate 2 English

Practice Papers
For SQA Exams

ENGLISH
INTERMEDIATE 2

**Exam B
Critical Essay**

Answer TWO questions from this paper.

You have 1 hour 30 minutes to complete this paper.

Each question must be chosen from a different Section (A–E). You are not allowed to choose two questions from the same Section.

In all Sections you may use Scottish texts.

Write the number of each question in the margin of your answer booklet and begin each essay on a fresh page.

You should spend about 45 minutes on each essay.

The following will be assessed:

- the relevance of your essays to the questions you have chosen

- your knowledge and understanding of key elements, central concerns and significant details of the chosen texts

- your explanation of ways in which aspects of structure/style/language contribute to the meaning/effect/impact of the chosen texts

- your evaluation of the effectiveness of the chosen texts, supported by detailed and relevant evidence

- the quality and technical accuracy of your writing.

25 marks are allocated to each question. The total for this paper is 50 marks.

Scotland's leading educational publishers

SECTION A – DRAMA

Your answer should make reference to your chosen text and to such elements as theme, structure, characterisation, plot, setting, key scene(s), conflict, climax….

1. Choose a play in which **two** characters hold opposing values.

   Briefly describe the characters and their values and explain how the conflict of these values affected the development of their relationship **or** what effect the conflict of these values had on the outcome of the play.

2. Choose a play where in **one** scene a character realises something important about his/her own character **or** situation.

   Say how this realisation came about and how this scene affects the unfolding of following events **or** affects his/her self-image.

3. Choose a play with a theme which you feel is important to 21st-century society.

   State what the theme is and show how the writer's handling of it deepened your understanding of this theme.

SECTION B – PROSE

Your answer should make reference to your chosen text and to such elements as theme, setting, key incident(s), plot, characterisation, structure, language, ideas, narrative technique, climax/turning point, description….

4. Choose a novel or short story which features an unattractive character.

   Describe the part played by him/her and show how the author sustains your interest in this character.

5. Choose a novel or short story with an opening section which creates a powerful atmosphere.

   Say how this effect was achieved and show how it helped prepare you for the presentation of a character **or** a theme.

6. Choose a prose work (fiction or non-fiction) which effectively illustrates a society/culture in a time other than the present.

   Describe the impact of this society/culture on you and say by what means this effect was created.

SECTION C – POETRY

> Your answer should make reference to your chosen text and to such elements as content, structure, theme, rhythm, word choice, sound, tone, ideas, imagery....

7. Choose a poem which views an experience/event through a child's eyes.

   Show the techniques by which this experience was re-created for you and say what effect they have on your response to the poem.

8. Choose a poem with a strong sense of place.

   Briefly describe the scene and then show how the techniques employed made this sense of place clear to you.

9. Choose a poem written in ballad or sonnet form.

   Explain **either** how the technical features of the poem added to your enjoyment of the poem **or** how the poet used the form to give shape to his/her material.

SECTION D – FILM AND TV DRAMA

> Your answer should make reference to your chosen text and to such elements as plot, characterisation, use of camera, editing, *mise-en-scène*, setting, dialogue, music/sound effects, key sequence....

10. Choose a film or TV drama (including a single play, a serial or a series) in which you are expected to like **or** dislike a certain character.

    Examine the techniques the director has used to shape our response to this character and say how effective you found these means.

11. Choose a key scene or sequence from a film or TV drama (including a single play, a serial or a series) which changes your earlier view of a situation **or** a character.

    Briefly describe how your view changed and say what techniques were employed to bring about this change.

12. Choose a film or TV drama (including a single play, a serial or a series) in which a familiar genre (Epic, Horror, Science Fiction, Western, Soap Opera, etc.) is transformed in some way by the director.

    State what changes are made to the traditional genre markers and say what effect these changes have on you.

SECTION E – LANGUAGE

Answers to questions in this section should refer to the text and to such relevant features as register, accent, dialect, slang, jargon, vocabulary, tone, abbreviation....

13. Consider the language of a leaflet, brochure or advertisement seeking your support for a cause **or** a product.

    By referring to this text, explore the various techniques used to seek the support and assess their success.

14. Consider the spoken language of teenagers.

    By referring to specific speech examples, say how their language differs from standard usage. Outline the advantages and disadvantages teenagers may derive from this language.

15. Consider the language of text messaging.

    By referring to specific examples, explain how its usage may aid or hinder communication.

[End of Question Paper]

Practice Exam C

Practice Paper C: Intermediate 2 English

Practice Papers
For SQA Exams

ENGLISH
INTERMEDIATE 2

Exam C
Close Reading

Answer all of the questions.

You have 1 hour to complete this paper.

Read the following passage and then answer the questions. Remember to use your own words as much as possible.

The questions ask you to show that you:

understand the ideas and details in the passage – **what the writer has said**
(**U**: Understanding)

can identify the techniques the writer has used to express these ideas – **how it has been said**
(**A**: Analysis)

can comment on how effective the writer has been, using appropriate evidence from the passage – **how well it has been said**
(**E**: Evaluation)

The code letters (U, A, E) are next to each question to make sure you know the question's purpose. The number of marks per question will give you a good idea as to how long your answer should be.

BUY, BUY BABY

In her book Buy, Buy Baby *the writer Susan Gregory Thomas describes how American companies market their products to very young children and their parents.*

In the majority of American households with children between the ages of zero and three years old, popping in a baby video or flicking on the TV set to a preschool programme is as mundane a routine as tooth-brushing or bathtime. It is not so much a parenting decision as a national reflex. Such videos and TV programmes are

5   marketed as educational for babies and toddlers, and it is generally accepted that on some level they are educational. Noggin, a cable channel for preschoolers, touts its tag-line: 'It's Like Preschool on TV'. There's little reason to question that claim. The channel was started as a joint venture of Nickelodeon and Sesame Workshop, both trustworthy institutions. Many preschoolers have mastered mousing skills by

10   their second birthday, and the web-sites of their favourite shows have games and activities for toddlers. The term 'preschooler' is understood by many sources to refer to two- to five-year olds; some include eighteen-month olds in that category.

Elitists may find it tacky, but few Americans – and not just parents of very young children – register it as unusual that at chain bookstores and libraries, many of

15   the most popular books for infants and toddlers are based on licensed television characters or snack foods. Many of these programmes are produced in collaboration with Scholastic, a company whose reputation is synonymous with education. There is little reason to question the claims by makers of baby toys and equipment that their products 'stimulate' babies' cognitive abilities with blinking lights or classical music.

20   The packaging explains why such features are educational, and parents are sure that they read or saw something that an expert said about them. In any case, most people buy these products because that's what is on the market.

The world of infants and toddlers did not look like this even fifteen years ago. Babies and toddlers were generally used by the media only as stars in daytime television

25   commercials (enter the wobbly tot, lurching around the house as a frazzled mother follows with a roll of paper towels and a happy defeated smile for her irresistible little monster). Mothers were the target consumers. Very young children were simply considered too young to grasp basic advertising pitches; moreover, the industry generally viewed pushing products on little children as un-ethical. But much has

30   changed in a very short time. Until very recently, for example, 'preschooler' referred to four- and five-year olds; those younger than three were considered babies or toddlers. Today the 'zero-to-three' market has become the first segment in 'cradle-to-grave' marketing, representing more than $20 billion a year. Selling to this age group is a rapidly growing industry manned by a battalion of specialised and sophisticated

35   advertising firms; child psychology researchers, often funded by companies interested in building a consumer base of very young children; and cross-marketing campaigns that deliberately intertwine educational messages with subtle commercial ploys. As the zero-to-three market has grown, so has a popular culture revolving around babies and toddlers. It includes formal classes and school (gymnastics, music, art, academics),

40   the use of machines previously reserved for adults and older kids (computers, VCRs, TV, DVRs, cell phones, digital cameras), and rigorous schedules to ensure that every moment offers an opportunity to 'learn'.

The emergence of the zero-to-three market has, both directly and indirectly, compelled the toy, food and apparel industries as well as every major media conglomerate, to

45 reconfigure their long-term marketing strategies. Brand recognition starts much earlier than one might think. Marketing studies show that children can discern brands as early as eighteen months; by twenty-four months they ask for products by brand name. In fact, a study conducted in 2000 found that brands wield as much influence on two-year-olds as they used to on children of five and up. Nearly two-

50 thirds of the mothers interviewed for the study reported that their children asked for specific brands before the age of three, while one-third said their kids were aware of brands at age two or earlier. Brands that kids knew best included Cheerio's, Disney, McDonald's, Pop-Tarts, Coke and Barbie.

The phenomenon of cradle-to-grave marketing can, in some ways, be seen as the

55 ultimate, inevitable step in the phenomenon that kids' marketers have long referred to as KGOY: Kids Getting Older Younger. Since the 1980s, marketers have been refining ways of mining the 'tween' market; children between the ages of six and eleven. This age group has always been brand-conscious, but as one long-time marketer put it, 'It's dribbled down' to even younger children. But how has this

60 happened and why?

If any one event triggered this neurosis, it was the 1997 White House Conference on Early Childhood Development and Learning, later famously referred to as the 'brain conference'. The conference called on experts in the field of early childhood development to explain how the brain grows during the first three years of life.

65 Presenters emphasised that the brain develops more rapidly, and makes more significant connections, than it ever will again.

From *Buy, Buy Baby* by Susan Gregory Thomas

QUESTIONS

1. Look again at lines 1 to 3.

Write down **two** words or phrases from the opening sentence which tell you that watching a baby video or television programme is normal in many American households. 2U

2. Look again at lines 3 to 6.

Explain **in your own words** the expression 'not so much a parenting decision as a national reflex'. 2U

3. Look again at lines 6 and 7.

What is the writer's **attitude** towards the company's tag-line in the sentence 'Noggin, a cable channel for pre-schoolers, touts its tag-line: "It's Like Preschool on TV"'? **Quote** to support your answer. 2A

4. Look again at lines 16 and 17.

In your own words, explain how consumers feel about the company Scholastic. Write down **one** word from paragraph 1 which conveys the same idea about other organisations. 2U

5. Look again at lines 17 to 22.

In your own words, explain the **three** reasons the writer gives for why parents buy baby toys and equipment which '"stimulate" babies' cognitive abilities'. 3U

6. Look again at lines 23 to 27.

Comment on the writer's **word choice** when describing *(a)* the child and *(b)* the mother who might appear in daytime television commercials. 4A

7. Look again at lines 27 to 29.

Why were very young children not considered to be target consumers previously? **Answer in your own words**. 2U

8. Look again at lines 29 to 30.

Comment on the **function** of the word 'But' in 'But much has changed in a very short time.' 2A

9. Look again at lines 33 to 35.

Comment on the effectiveness of the **imagery** used in the phrase 'a rapidly growing industry manned by a battalion of specialised and sophisticated advertising firms' to convey the writer's view of advertising firms. 2A

10. Look again at lines 39 and 42.

Why does the writer use **inverted commas** around the word 'learn'? 1A

11. Look again at lines 45 to 53.

Identify and explain **one** example of evidence the writer gives to show that brand recognition starts 'earlier than you might think'. 2U

12. Look again at line 56.

Explain fully how the phrase 'Kids Getting Older Younger' achieves its impact.

2A

13. Look again at lines 61 to 66.

In your opinion, why might the White House Conference in 1997 have made parents interested in buying 'educational' products for their children? **Quote** to support your answer.

2U

14. Think about the passage as a whole.

The writer's main argument is that marketers target both very young children and their parents in order to sell more products. How **persuasive** do you find her argument? Justify your answer fully.

2E

Total (30)

[End of Question Paper]

Practice Paper C: Intermediate 2 English

Practice Papers
For SQA Exams

ENGLISH
INTERMEDIATE 2

Exam C
Critical Essay

Answer TWO questions from this paper.

You have 1 hour 30 minutes to complete this paper.

Each question must be chosen from a different Section (A–E). You are not allowed to choose two questions from the same Section.

In all Sections you may use Scottish texts.

Write the number of each question in the margin of your answer booklet and begin each essay on a fresh page.

You should spend about 45 minutes on each essay.

The following will be assessed:

- the relevance of your essays to the questions you have chosen

- your knowledge and understanding of key elements, central concerns and significant details of the chosen texts

- your explanation of ways in which aspects of structure/style/language contribute to the meaning /effect/impact of the chosen texts

- your evaluation of the effectiveness of the chosen texts, supported by detailed and relevant evidence

- the quality and technical accuracy of your writing.

25 marks are allocated to each question. The total for this paper is 50 marks.

SECTION A – DRAMA

> Your answer should make reference to your chosen text and to such elements as theme, structure, characterisation, plot, setting, key scene(s), conflict, climax....

1. Choose a play in which a character encounters a disappointment or a setback.

   Explain how this disappointment or setback came about and say how it affected his/her fate in the rest of the play.

2. Choose a play with a scene in which a theme is made particularly clear.

   State what this theme is and explain how the author deepened your understanding of this theme in your chosen scene.

3. Choose a play in which an important relationship comes under strain.

   Show why this strain came about and explain how this strain was resolved and its effect on the outcome of the play.

SECTION B – PROSE

> Your answer should make reference to your chosen text and to such elements as theme, setting, key incident(s), plot, characterisation, structure, language, ideas, narrative technique, climax/turning point, description....

4. Choose a novel or short story in which your approval of **or** sympathy towards a character increases as the narrative proceeds.

   Describe how your reaction to this character changes, explaining the techniques the author employed to bring about this change.

5. Choose a prose work (fiction or non-fiction) that deals with a topic with which you were unfamiliar.

   Show how the writer presents this topic and explain how the topic was made interesting for you **or** what this text taught you.

6. Choose a novel or short story with an incident which makes clear an aspect of a main character which you found unexpected.

   Describe the incident. Show how this incident was important in helping you to understand this character better.

SECTION C – POETRY

> Your answer should make reference to your chosen text and to such elements as content, structure, theme, rhythm, word choice, sound, tone, ideas, imagery....

7. Choose a poem which deals with a topic affecting family members or society in general.

   Show how the poet's use of content and poetic techniques helped to increase your understanding of the topic **or** made the ideas under discussion memorable.

8. Choose a poem which appeals to you for its effective use of poetic techniques to explore an experience **or** a place **or** an emotion in a way that caught your interest.

   Describe the techniques employed and say how their use deepened your understanding of the poet's reaction to the experience, place or emotion.

9. Choose a poem which invites you to consider a happy **or** unhappy event or experience.

   Explain how the emotion of this event or experience was conveyed by the poet and say what you learned about the topic from the poet's treatment of it.

SECTION D – FILM AND TV DRAMA

> Your answer should make reference to your chosen text and to such elements as plot, characterisation, use of camera, editing, *mise-en-scène*, setting, dialogue, music/sound effects, key sequence....

10. Choose a film or TV drama (including a single play, a serial or a series) which deals with modern warfare or violence in society.

    Explain how your chosen film or TV drama deals with modern warfare or violence in society by its choice of content and the techniques employed.

11. Choose a film or TV drama (including a play, serial or a series) in which a scene or sequence effectively establishes a key character or theme.

    Briefly describe the scene or sequence and explain the techniques used to capture your interest in the character or theme.

12. Choose a film or TV drama (including a single play, a serial or a series) in which a character's past influences his/her present character or actions.

    Briefly describe why the past is so important in the character's life and discuss the media techniques used to reveal its importance to the audience.

SECTION E – LANGUAGE

> Answers to questions in this section should refer to the text and to such relevant features as register, accent, dialect, slang, jargon, vocabulary, tone, abbreviation....

13. Consider the spoken language of your locality **or** a particular geographical area you know well.

    By referring to specific examples, say how this language sets itself apart from Standard English and say what advantages and/or disadvantages it offers its speakers.

14. Consider the language used by a newspaper with which you are familiar when reporting on sport **or** war **or** crime.

    Referring to specific examples, describe what is distinctive about this language and say how effective you find it to be.

15. Consider two advertisements you consider to be effectively persuasive in their different ways.

    Refer in detail to the differences in their use of language and say what makes the approach in each one distinctive and effective.

Practice Exam D

Practice Paper D: Intermediate 2 English

Practice Papers
For SQA Exams

ENGLISH
INTERMEDIATE 2

Exam D
Close Reading

Answer all of the questions.

You have 1 hour to complete this paper.

Read the following passage and then answer the questions. Remember to use your own words as much as possible.

The questions ask you to show that you:

understand the ideas and details in the passage – **what the writer has said**
(**U**: Understanding)

can identify the techniques the writer has used to express these ideas – **how it has been said**
(**A**: Analysis)

can comment on how effective the writer has been, using appropriate evidence from the passage – **how well it has been said**
(**E**: Evaluation)

The code letters (U, A, E) are next to each question to make sure you know the question's purpose. The number of marks per question will give you a good idea as to how long your answer should be.

DRY STOREROOM NO. 1: THE SECRET LIFE OF THE NATURAL HISTORY MUSEUM

In Richard Fortey's book Dry Storeroom No. 1: The Secret Life of the Natural History Museum, *the writer describes his work as a scientist at the Natural History Museum in London.*

This book is my own storeroom, a personal archive, designed to explain what goes on behind the polished doors in the Natural History Museum. All our lives are collections curated through memory. We pick up recollections and facts and store them, often half forgotten, or tucked away on shelves buried deep in the psyche. Not everything
5 is as blameless as we might like. But the sum total of that deep archive is what makes us who we are. I cannot escape the fact that working for a whole lifetime within the extravagant building in South Kensington has moulded much of my character. By the same token, I also know the place rather better than any outsider.

I believe profoundly in the importance of museums; I would go as far as to say that you
10 can judge a society by the quality of its museums. But they do not exist as collections alone. In the long term, the lustre of a museum does not depend only on the artefacts or objects it contains – the people who work out of sight are what keeps a museum alive by contributing research to make the collections active, or by applying learning and scholarship to reveal more than was known before about the stored objects.

15 At first glance the Natural History Museum looks like some kind of cathedral, dominated by towers topped by short spires; these lie at the centre of the building and at its eastern and western corners. Even on a dull day the outside of the Museum shows a pleasing shade of buff, a mass of terracotta tiles, the warmth of which contrasts with the pale stucco of the terraces that line much of the other side of
20 the Cromwell Road. Courses of blue tiles break up the solidity of the façade. The entrance to the Museum is a great rounded repeated arch, flanked by columns, and the front doors are reached by walking up a series of broad steps.

The main hall still retains the feel of the nave of a great Gothic cathedral because it is so high and generously vaulted. Many visitors, and most children, don't even
25 notice the charming ceiling paintings. Their attention is captured by other bones: the enormous *Diplodocus* dinosaur that occupies the centre of the ground floor, heading in osteological splendour towards the door. Its tiny head bears a mouthful of splayed teeth in a grinning welcome.

Diplodocus was proudly in place when I first came to the Natural History Museum
30 as a little boy in the 1950s, and it was still there when I retired in 2006. I am always glad to see it; not that I regard a constructed replica of an ancient fossil as an old friend, it is just consoling to pass the time of day with something that changes little in a mutable world.

But *Diplodocus has* changed, albeit rather subtly. When I was a youngster, the
35 enormously long *Diplodocus* tail hung down at the rear end and almost trailed along the floor, its great number of extended vertebrae supported by a series of little props. This arrangement was not popular with the warders, as unscrupulous visitors would occasionally steal the last vertebra from the end of the tail. There was even a box of "spares" to make good the work of thieves so that the full backbone was restored by
40 the time the doors opened the following day. Visitors today will see a rather different

Diplodocus: the tail is elevated like an extended whip held well above the ground, supported on a brass crutch which has been somewhat cruelly compared with those often to be found in the paintings of Salvador Dalí; now the massive beast has an altogether more vigorous stance. The skeleton was remodelled after research indicated
45 that the tail had a function as a counterbalance to the extraordinarily long neck at the opposite end of the body. Far from being a laggard, *Diplodocus* was an active animal, despite the smallness of its brain. Nowadays, all the huge sauropod dinosaurs in films such as *Jurassic Park* show the tail in this active position. Many exhibits in a natural history museum are not permanent in the way that sculptures or portraits are in an
50 art gallery. Bones can be rehung in a more literal way than paintings.

Now animatronic dinosaurs flash their teeth and groan, and carry us back effectively to the Cretaceous period, a hundred million years ago. Small children shelter nervously behind the legs of their parents. "Don't worry," say the parents, "they aren't real." The kids do not always look convinced. There is, to my mind, still something eloquent
55 about the *Diplodocus* specimen: not merely its size, but that it is the assembled evidence for part of a vanished world. All those glamorous animations and movie adventures rely ultimately on the bones. A museum is a place where the visitor can come to examine evidence, as well as to be diverted. Before the exhibitions started to tell stories, that was one of the main functions of a museum, and the evidence was
60 laid out in ranks. There are still galleries in the Natural History Museum displaying minerals, the objects themselves – unadorned but for labels – a kind of museum of a museum, preserved in aspic from the days of such systematic rather than thematic exhibits. Few people now find their way to these galleries.

The public galleries take up much less than half of the space of the Natural History
65 Museum. Tucked away, mostly out of view, there is a warren of corridors, obsolete galleries, offices, libraries and above all, collections. This is the natural habitat of the curator. It is where I have spent a large part of my life – indeed, the Natural History Museum provides a way of life as distinctive as that of a monastery. Most people in the world at large know very little about this unique habitat. This is the world I shall
70 reveal.

From *Dry Storeroom No. 1: The Secret Life of the Natural History Museum*
by Richard Fortey

QUESTIONS

1. Look again at the first sentence.

    According to the writer, what will the book be about? **Quote** to support your
    answer.   2U

2. Look again at lines 3 to 4.

    Identify **one technique** used by the writer to convey how 'recollections and
    facts' are stored, and comment on its effectiveness.   2A

3. Look again at lines 9 and 10.

Write down **two** expressions which show that the writer feels strongly about museums and their importance.   2U

4. Look again at line 11.

'Lustre' means 'shine' or 'gloss'. Explain fully why this is an appropriate **word choice** in this context.   2A

5. Look again at lines 11 to 14.

Explain **in your own words** what people who work in museums do to keep a museum 'alive'.   2U

6. Look again at lines 17 to 20.

Write down **two** expressions from the sentences 'Even on a dull day the outside of the Museum shows a pleasing shade of buff, a mass of terracotta tiles, the warmth of which contrasts with the pale stucco of the terraces that line much of the other side of the Cromwell Road. Courses of blue tiles break up the solidity of the façade' to show that the writer thinks the Natural History Museum is an attractive building.   2U

7. Look again at lines 23 to 28.

In what way does the first sentence of this paragraph **link** with the previous paragraph?   2A

8. Look again at lines 23 to 28.

Explain why visitors might not notice the ceiling paintings. **Quote** to support your answer.   2U

9. Look again at lines 29 to 33.

What is the writer's **attitude** towards the dinosaur skeleton when he sees it? Answer **in your own words**.   2U

10. Look again at lines 34 to 46.

In your own words, why have changes been made to the *Diplodocus'* tail?   2U

11. Look again at line 54.

Comment on the writer's **word choice** in the phrase 'The kids do not always look convinced'. 2A

12. Look again at lines 57 to 60.

Explain **in your own words** the **two** main functions of a museum before they 'started to tell stories'. 2U

13. Look again at line 61.

Explain why the writer uses **dashes** around the phrase 'unadorned but for labels'. 2A

14. Look again at lines 66 to 67.

How appropriate is the writer's **word choice** in the sentence 'This is the natural habitat of the curator'? Explain your answer fully. 2A

15. Think about the passage as a whole.

In your opinion, what is the writer's **main purpose** in writing this book; to inform **or** to persuade? Give reasons for your answer. 2E

Total (30)

[End of Question Paper]

Practice Paper D: Intermediate 2 English

Practice Papers
For SQA Exams

ENGLISH
INTERMEDIATE 2

Exam D
Critical Essay

Answer TWO questions from this paper.

You have 1 hour 30 minutes to complete this paper.

Each question must be chosen from a different Section (A–E). You are not allowed to choose two questions from the same Section.

In all Sections you may use Scottish texts.

Write the number of each question in the margin of your answer booklet and begin each essay on a fresh page.

You should spend about 45 minutes on each essay.

The following will be assessed:

- the relevance of your essays to the questions you have chosen

- your knowledge and understanding of key elements, central concerns and significant details of the chosen texts

- your explanation of ways in which aspects of structure/style/language contribute to the meaning /effect/impact of the chosen texts

- your evaluation of the effectiveness of the chosen texts, supported by detailed and relevant evidence

- the quality and technical accuracy of your writing.

25 marks are allocated to each question. The total for this paper is 50 marks.

SECTION A – DRAMA

Your answer should make reference to your chosen text and to such elements as theme, structure, characterisation, plot, setting, key scene(s), conflict, climax….

1. Choose a character from a play for whom the outcome of the play – happy **or** unhappy – is deserved in your opinion.

   Describe briefly what befalls this character and explain how the author's presentation of this character helped you reach this opinion.

2. Choose a play in which a chief concern is either prejudice **or** jealousy **or** ambition **or** obsession.

   Say what the concern is and go on to show how the author treats this concern in a way that deepened your understanding of its workings.

3. Choose a play with a memorable final scene.

   Briefly describe the scene and the reasons for its appeal to you, discussing how the techniques used by the author helped establish the scene's power.

SECTION B – PROSE

Your answer should make reference to your chosen text and to such elements as theme, setting, key incident(s), plot, characterisation, structure, language, ideas, narrative technique, climax/turning point, description….

4. Choose a novel or short story in which the author appears to be criticising some aspect of our society **or** society of an earlier age.

   Describe the criticism as it emerges in the text, saying how the author persuades us to share his/her view of this aspect of the society in question.

5. Choose a prose work (fiction or non-fiction) which deals with an important issue such as racial intolerance **or** scientific discovery **or** social inequality.

   Identify the issue, before going on to explain how the author dealt with the subject in a way that helped you understand it more fully.

6. Choose a novel or short story in which not a great deal happens and yet your interest was caught.

Briefly describe the content of the text and identify by what means the author made the text interesting.

SECTION C – POETRY

Your answer should make reference to your chosen text and to such elements as content, structure, theme, rhythm, word choice, sound, tone, ideas, imagery....

7. Choose a poem whose subject **or** setting **or** speaker held a strong appeal for you.

Briefly describe the poem and say how the poet's skills helped create this appeal.

8. Choose a poem written in Scots.

Say how the use of this language affected your enjoyment of the poem.

9. Choose a poem which tells a story.

Outline the events and describe the techniques used by the poet to engage your interest in them.

SECTION D – FILM AND TV DRAMA

Your answer should make reference to your chosen text and to such elements as plot, characterisation, use of camera, editing, *mise-en-scène*, setting, dialogue, music/sound effects, key sequence....

10. Choose a film or TV drama (including a single play, a serial or a series) in which humour was used to make a serious point(s) about society or relationships.

Briefly describe the contribution of humour and how it affected your understanding of the theme(s) and/or characters.

11. Choose a film or TV drama (including a single play, a serial or a series) with a Scottish setting.

Show how the director set about creating his view of Scotland and say how effective you found its presentation **or** explain how the setting added to your enjoyment of the film or TV drama.

12. Choose a film with a character who is unfortunate in some way.

Describe the character and explain the means used by the director to enlist your sympathy for the character.

SECTION E – LANGUAGE

Answers to questions in this section should refer to the text and to such relevant features as register, accent, dialect, slang, jargon, vocabulary, tone, abbreviation....

13. Consider how advances in technology have created a distinctive language for electronic communications.

Choose an electronic medium (sms/text, blogs, email, etc.). By referring to specific examples from your chosen medium, explain how traditional language has been affected, suggesting any benefits or disadvantages the changes have brought users.

14. Consider the language of graphic novels.

What aspects of dialogue and narrative are distinctive to the genre and what advantages and/or disadvantages are offered over the language of conventional novels?

15. Consider the language of product advertising aimed at teenagers in the press or in the electronic media.

By referring to specific examples, discuss popular persuasive techniques employed, suggesting how effective you find them in targeting their audience.

[End of Question Paper]

Worked Answers

PRACTICE PAPER A   CLOSE READING WORKED ANSWERS

Note: alternative answers are shown by the symbol /. Where the alternative answer is longer, it may also be shown after the word OR.

1. It 'has a knack for distortion' (1 mark) which means time changes or twists what we remember (1 mark). OR 'fogging the images from the past' (1 mark) tells us that we may not remember things or events clearly (1 mark). OR

   'making everything feel bigger than it really was' (1 mark) means our memories may be exaggerated or unrealistic (1 mark). OR 'messing with the collage of mental snapshots' (1 mark) means we may not remember things or events in the right order/clearly (1 mark).

   > **TOP EXAM TIP**
   >
   > Always copy carefully when you are quoting from the passage. If you quote wrongly or do not spell the quote correctly, it may not be clear to the examiner that you have identified the correct quote – and you may lose marks.

   > *HINT* There are plenty of phrases to choose from here. Using a highlighter helps you to highlight key words and phrases. Here you gain one mark for a correct quote and one mark for explaining this in your own words.

2. What happened had an effect on him/affected him/was powerful for him (1 mark) AND what happened has stayed with him for a long time/has lasted (1 mark).

   > *HINT* You are being asked here to explain the phrase 'its enduring influence' which appears towards the end of the sentence. One mark is for explaining 'enduring' and one mark is for explaining 'influence'.

   > **TOP EXAM TIP**
   >
   > Use a highlighter to highlight key words in the passage. Don't forget that highlighting w...

   [handwritten note: It a sentence looks odd, think why? what is the writer's intention?]

3. The sentence starts with 'Quite why' (1 mark) AND this emph... writer does not understand the reason for taking the poodle o... (1 mark).

   > *HINT* Here you gain one mark for identifying what is unusual about the sentence structure and one mark for explaining the effect of this. Did you spot that the phrase 'I will never know' would normally be placed at the beginning of the sentence? Placing words or phrases at the beginning of a sentence (or the end) emphasises them, making them more important.

   [handwritten note: Think about emphasis.]

4. Any one from:

   'staring' the writer down (1 mark) OR 'defending' his space (1 ma... a 'snarl'/'wrinkle' (1 mark) which shows that the poodle is aggres... writer (1 mark).

   OR any one from:

   'feigning innocence' (1 mark) OR 'doe-eyed stares' (1 mark), which shows that the poodle pretends to have done nothing when the writer complains to Grandma (1 mark).

   > *HINT* There is one mark here for explaining how the poodle behaves and one mark for quoting correctly. Quote any word or phrase which shows the poodle's aggression towards the writer or innocence when Grandma is involved.

5. 'ominous-looking' means worrying or threatening or suspicious (1 mark) AND the word 'threat' helps me to work this out as it has the same meaning (1 mark).

TOP EXAM TIP

The context – that is, the words and phrases which surround a specific word or phrase – usually helps you to work out the meaning of a phrase you may not know. Look for words or phrases or ideas that may give a clue as to what a word or phrase means.

HINT

Here, the writer describes 'ominous-looking clouds' then 'the threat of rain'. One mark is for giving the correct meaning and one mark is for explaining (and quoting from) the context.

6. 'having the time of his life' (1 mark) AND 'He didn't even mind that I was holding Grandma's hand' (1 mark).

HINT

Look through the paragraph to find examples of Marty using human behaviours or actions.

7. Any two from: 'the surf crashing hard' OR 'quite a pull' OR 'icy cold'.

HINT

There are plenty of examples here for one mark each. You will gain no marks for 'not swimming weather' OR' not paddling weather' as these phrases do not convey that the sea is dangerous. Always read the question carefully; you are asked to find words or phrases **before** Marty disappears.

8. The function of this sentence is to link the events of the previous paragraphs (1 mark) with the paragraphs which follow (1 mark).

HINT

You may be asked about the function of a sentence, phrase, word or idea. Here you are asked about a phrase. The function of a phrase means what it does. Of course, you also need to know what it means so that you can explain what it links! As you have already read the whole passage, you know that this sentence refers to the moment the dog disappears – the passage has described events leading up to this and then describes events after it.

9. The writer uses understatement in 'I couldn't swim'/'my mother had not packed my inflatable rubber ring' (1 mark) as he is stating very simply/directly/with no exaggeration that he cannot take action in this crisis situation (1 mark).

OR

The writer uses exaggeration (1 mark) in 'a selfless, heroic act' to create humour by overstatement (1 mark).

HINT

Understatement is often used to create a humorous effect; a writer states very simply something that would normally be expressed more strongly or in a more complex way. Humour can also be created through exaggeration. Sometimes understatement and exaggeration are used together to create a contrast – did you spot that both are used here?

10. Any two from:

The writer could have behaved badly/cruelly/evilly (1 mark).

AND/OR

The writer could have watched the dog disappearing without telling anyone (1 mark).

AND/OR

The writer could have diverted everyone's/Grandma's attention so that the dog was not saved (1 mark).

HINT Here you gain one mark for each explanation about what the writer could have done. There is some challenging vocabulary here. Read carefully and slowly using your highlighter to find the possible answers.

11. 'Don't worry' OR 'what really happened' OR 'Bear in mind' OR 'like she was all lubed up' (1 mark).

AND

The writer uses this informal language to engage the reader/to address the reader directly/to make the tone conversational/as he is 'telling a story'/to create humour (1 mark).

HINT Use a highlighter to find examples of informal language. Remember that abbreviations, use of dialect or slang words, grammatically incorrect expressions are all examples of informality. Practise spotting formal and informal words and phrases so that you know the difference. Think about situations when you would use formal language (for example, an application letter) and informal language (for example, when chatting to your friends).

12. The mother tells off/scolds/shouts at the grandmother (1 mark) AND/OR the mother treats the grandmother as a child (1 mark) AND/OR the grandmother behaves like a child (1 mark).

HINT Role reversal means to switch roles or to behave in the opposite way to how people behave normally. Did you spot all three examples?

13. The paragraph is short/contains only one sentence/summarises in one sentence (1 mark) and this makes it stand out/emphasises what has taken place (1 mark).

OR

The paragraph contains humour/exaggeration (1 mark) as the writer suggests the dog has been 'sent by the devil' to frighten children (1 mark).

HINT You are being asked here about the writer's craft. You can choose to comment on the sentence structure or on the writer's word choice. Which did you choose?

TOP EXAM TIP

All **analysis** questions ask you about the writer's craft. Writer's craft includes all the techniques the writer uses to create an impact on the reader. Usually, you are asked about one specific technique, for example, imagery or sentence structure. Sometimes you are asked to identify and comment on the technique used.

14. The writer is unwilling/unable to believe what happened (1 mark).

AND

The writer became aware of/learned about the strong relationship between the dog and his grandmother (1 mark).

HINT Here you are asked to explain 'incredulity over an unthinkable rescue' and 'a realization that something mysterious and powerful was at work'. You must explain the two points clearly here for two marks.

15. I think the writer does change his attitude (1 mark) as he realises that the grandmother and dog have a very strong bond (1 mark) OR as he now finds the dog 'pathetic' and not 'menacing' (1 mark).

OR

I think the writer does not change his attitude (1 mark) as he still dislikes the dog despite realising that the grandmother loves it (1 mark).

> **HINT** All evaluation questions are asking for your opinion. So here you can agree or disagree that the writer's attitude changes. Always include justification from the passage for your opinion either by explaining in your own words or by quoting from the passage directly.

PRACTICE PAPER A — CRITICAL ESSAY WORKED ANSWERS

EXAM ANSWER ADVICE

In theory, you have 45 minutes to write each critical essay. In practice, however, you have somewhat less time since you have first to:

(a) select the two questions which you feel you are competent to answer.

(b) reflect on the full implications of the wording of the question by underlining what you see as key words.

(c) plan your material to fit the wording of the question.

Do not allow yourself to be panicked into writing the essay right away; a little time spent on these three stages will result in a much more convincing answer.

In reflecting on the question and planning your answer, remember that the wording of the question comes in two blocks, with the second part usually inviting you to perform two tasks, e.g. *Describe the relationship up to this point ... then show the effect this change ...* It is critically important to balance out your answer over these two parts. Do not spend most of your time on the first part and then discover you have two minutes to consider the second part.

TOP EXAM TIP

As you write, try from time to time to weave parts of the wording of the question into your answer. This helps show the examiner you are answering the question. More importantly, it keeps you on task and helps you to present a consistent line of reasoned thought, rather than a series of unconnected points. *But if lack of formal education **increases our sympathy** for Rita, so too does the opposition she faces from her husband.*

Section A – Drama

EXAM ANSWER ADVICE

That text box before the list of drama questions is a handy reminder of the technical terms that help form an appropriate critical response.

Remember, too, that a play is a theatrical experience and your response needs to take in not only the content of the text, but the overall effect of this text on the audience as we watch the characters' progress. *As we watch we feel that ...*

1.

> **HINT** In explaining 'the reasons for this determination' you will have to select earlier facts from the character's situation which make clear what drives this determination, but be careful not to end up spending your time re-telling the plot. Select reasons carefully and support with evidence.

Having identified the driving force behind the determination, you will need to discuss the action(s) undertaken and show how these do or do not lead to happiness. This question would suit a number of very different plays: *Educating Rita, Macbeth, The Crucible, The Winslow Boy ...*

2.

> **HINT** You haven't really revised a play unless you can confidently discuss *in detail* what goes on in at least three key scenes. Usually these will be the opening and closing scenes and one where there is either a crisis or a turning point.

Identify the scene (*In Act 2 Scene 1...*), briefly discuss how it opens and closes, pointing out why this scene is important, what you see as significant in the relationship development here and any changes you note in the characters involved. Then spend time commenting on the outcome for both parties from this turning point onwards. Remember that in plays with large casts, the two characters in this scene may not be the only people affected.

3.

> **HINT** In questions of this kind spend some time at least explaining why this issue is of particular interest to young people. Don't assume the examiner will automatically see the connection.

Love, education, parental control could all be selected issues. Scenes in which varying viewpoints come into conflict, or scenes in which characters' feelings and opinions are revealed may figure prominently. Do not forget, however, to connect these revelations to *your* understanding of the issue. What did you learn from them? How was your understanding deepened?

Section B – Prose

> **EXAM ANSWER ADVICE**
>
> All exam questions need careful study, but questions in this section need more study than most. Prose works come in several forms in this exam: short story, novel, fiction, non-fiction. Be careful not to muddle your genres; if a question is limited to a novel, do not attempt to write about a short story. A question mentioning 'a prose work' is the only one which allows you to examine any of these prose genres. Check carefully before selecting.
>
> The text box reminds you of some of the technical terms which, if used appropriately throughout the text, will make your essay sound academically persuasive to examiners.
>
> A short story allows you room for micro-analysis, but in writing about a novel, ensure that you catch the broad sweep of the text by discussing character, conflict, themes, setting, narrative stance, etc.

4. This is a question which perhaps favours an autobiography or a novel of the kind such as L.P. Hartley's *The Go-Between*. Select two or three memories only and discuss them in detail, highlighting the impact events/experiences left on the narrator. Do not overlook the question's all-important second task; here it is *your* reaction to those memories that needs to be detailed.

> **TOP EXAM TIP**
>
> Remember when planning your essay that the SEEC format – Statement, Evidence, Explanation, Comment – is a good way to structure body paragraphs to ensure you present your ideas logically and effectively.

5. It is preferable in a question of this kind to select a limited number of examples of symbols and imagery and discuss them in depth, before moving on to the second part of the task. Avoid making a long list of symbols and imagery; you will not have the time to say in any meaningful way how they all relate to the development of the text's themes. Doors and windows, for instance, in *The Strange Case of Dr Jekyll and Mr Hyde* would be worth exploring. Or mist or fog in *The Woman in Black*.

6. Note that although you are being asked to discuss difficulties involving a community, a family or a relationship, the focus is on a single character. Obviously, the situation affects other people (so their actions and reactions will have to be noted), but the focus of the question is firmly on a single character. The difficulties discussed must be seen from his/her perspective. His/her setting, past history, experiences will all need examining for the second part of the task.

> **TOP EXAM TIP**
>
> Do not try to include everything your teacher has brought to your attention about a text. One of the many points an exam question aims to test is your ability to *select* information. Your ability to select only that information which is relevant to the question counts for a great deal. A scatter-gun approach will fail to impress an examiner.

Section C – Poetry

> **EXAM ANSWER ADVICE**
>
> The text box above the questions is a handy reminder of the terms that will find favour with examiners when used appropriately in your answer.
>
> In those cases where poems you have studied are relatively short, it is a good idea to memorise them. This will provide you with a readily accessible source of evidence for whatever technique you may wish to call on to answer the question.
>
> While detailed reference to the text may be acceptable as evidence in a longer prose work or play, in a poem it is vital to be able to conjure up exact quotations. It is difficult, after all, to discuss onomatopoeia without actually illustrating the sounds in question.

7.

> **HINT**
>
> This is a question which focuses on your knowledge of poetic techniques as well as a poem itself. Beware, however, of simply identifying a certain technique at work. A successful answer will always underline *how* the use of that particular technique and the relevant quotation *affects* the reader's response to the poem. *The alliteration on the letter 'r' in 'red, red erupted' makes me/the reader feel...*

Your answer will need to call on a considerable bank of quotations to illustrate how the narrator's response was signalled. Make sure you name some of the techniques listed in the text box above the poetry section. Be aware, too, that there may be shifts in the poet's moods and reactions. Be sure to refer to this.

8. In detailing the incident/experience referred to, try to weave into your text a few brief direct quotations from the poem itself. Once you have satisfactorily outlined the experience, begin to explain the ways in which the poet relates these incidents to deeper truths about the human condition. Make the link point by point; don't generalise. Poems which would be useful for this kind of question include 'Poem for my sister' by Liz Lochhead or 'Child with Pillar Box and Bin Bags' by Kathleen Jamie.

9.

> **HINT**
>
> A *brief* description of content and your response to this would be a useful starting point.

You need to be sure of what the poet is making use of in place of a fixed pattern of rhyme and rhythm. Is there, say, an extended metaphor at work here? How important is alliteration or onomatopoeia? Or does the poet avoid 'poetic' language entirely? If so, why? Does the poem rely perhaps on enjambment and if so, for what purpose? Choose what you think are the most important features, give quotations to show these features in action, then discuss the effect on your reading experience. If you have time, consider what would have been lost/gained had the poet used regular metre and rhyme.

Section D – Film and TV Drama

> **EXAM ANSWER ADVICE**
>
> There is a good deal of overlap in the language used to discuss film and TV drama and the language used for prose, poetry and plays. Such features as characterisation, themes, plot and narrative stance all have to be dealt with. But added to these are the subject-specific features listed in the text box above the questions. No serious answer can fail to use an appropriate selection of these terms.

10. Currently, there is no shortage of film and TV dramas in which supernatural elements penetrate everyday situations. Films such the *Twilight* series, or the TV series *Buffy the Vampire Slayer*, *Demons*, *Being Human*, *The Ghost Whisperer*, to name only a few, all offer opportunities to discuss how their directors combined the paranormal with the normal. Remember that discussing the media techniques used to portray the supernatural is not enough; you need to bring in a discussion of the features you would also mention in a theatre play: characterisation, theme, key incident(s), etc. Analysis of a key scene (or scenes) or incident(s) would prevent your answer becoming weakly generalised.

> **TOP EXAM TIP**
>
> Remember that the SEEC format which you can use in critical essays on drama, poetry and prose will also prove helpful in writing essays on film and TV drama.

11. Although the question foregrounds 'setting' and 'characterisation', your answer needs also to consider the production features mentioned in the text box above the questions. 'Consumer society' allows you a fairly broad choice of film and TV drama in which malls, stores, cafés, bars and hotels feature prominently. Ultimately, a good answer will evaluate the director's view of this society as depicted through setting and characterisation. Analysis of a key scene (or scenes) or incident(s) would prevent your answer becoming weakly generalised.

12. Often (although there are exceptions) this may be a scene or sequence set fairly near the opening of the drama in question, where the director is creating his setting. This answer will perhaps lean more to pure media features than the other two questions in this paper. Music, sound effects, camera angles, setting will sometimes be at work on your responses before any dialogue has been uttered. Remember a 'setting unfamiliar to you' can be interpreted as a scene from the past, the future or a present-day

> **TOP EXAM TIP**
>
> As in a good answer to a drama question, candidates opting for media questions should be prepared to discuss at least three key scenes or sequences from various points in the film *in some detail*. Make specific points about techniques at work and their effect on you. Generalisations will not convince.

life-style foreign to you for social, economic or geographic reasons. *Eragon*, *Clash of the Titans*, *Avatar*, the Harry Potter films, the Narnia films, 'The King's Speech', in their very different ways, could provide scenes or sequences which would prove useful for analysis.

Section E – Language

> **EXAM ANSWER ADVICE**
>
> These questions are best tackled only if you have used a Language text in class or if you have made a detailed study of various language varieties with your teacher. You must be prepared to analyse language in some detail, citing specific examples at work and interpreting their significance using the technical language indicated in the text box above the questions.

PRACTICE PAPER B   **CLOSE READING WORKED ANSWERS**

Note: alternative answers are shown by the symbol /. Where the alternative answer is longer, it may also be shown after the word OR.

1. He was not sure/was unsure that he wanted his family to be brought up/to develop into adults/to spend their childhood (1 mark) in America/behaving as Americans/adopting American habits/becoming American (1 mark).

> *HINT* This straightforward question is asking you to explain the phrase 'didn't think he liked the idea of his children growing up as Americans'. You must explain the idea of 'growing up' and the idea of 'in America' in your own words. No marks for using the word 'children'.

2. He describes the information as a 'gift' (1 mark), which means this information was special/precious/important/of value (1 mark). OR He describes the information as 'momentous' (1 mark), which means this information was very important or significant (1 mark).

> *HINT* Analysis questions ask you to look carefully at the language the writer has chosen to use. Here he uses the word 'gift' and the word 'momentous'. Your task is to analyse this word choice and explain why it has been used. Always think about the connotations of the words used. Connotation means the 'extra' meaning of a word, that is, all the associations a word has (beyond its basic dictionary definition). You need to make two clear points here for two marks.

TOP EXAM TIP

Questions always follow the order of the passage. Use the line numbers and the wording of the questions to help you locate the answer.

3. Any one from:

   Steve is an imaginary friend/alter ego/made up (1 mark).

   AND

   Steve is exactly the same age and appearance as Stephen (1 mark) OR Steve was 'born' as soon as Stephen found out the family nearly moved to America (1 mark) OR Stephen wanted very much to be American (1 mark).

> *HINT* Did you realise that Steve is not real? This gives you one mark. You gain a second mark for giving any correct reason, which can come from either the second or the third paragraph. You can include a quote if you wish, but you do not have to as you are not asked to 'quote to support your answer'.

4. Stephen was sometimes shy and sometimes confident (1 mark) AND/OR Stephen's personality changed suddenly (1 mark) AND/OR Stephen did not persuade others he was either shy or a show off (1 mark).

> *HINT* 'Veer' means to turn or swerve or change direction suddenly. 'Unconvincing' means unbelievable or implausible or not persuasive. You are being asked here to explain 'veered unconvincingly between shyness and showing off'. Note you do not have to answer in your own words so you can use the words 'shy'/'shyness' and 'show off'/'showing off' in your answer. There are two parts to the answer – one mark for explaining 'veered' and one mark for explaining 'unconvincingly'.

5. He wants to understand Americans' life-styles/lives/to get to know the country fully (1 mark)

AND

because he does not just want to know what it looks like/about outward appearances (1 mark) OR because he nearly grew up in America (1 mark).

> *HINT* — The answer to this question comes before and after the phrase 'but I (perhaps because of my father's decision) am interested in something more'. Lines 17 and 18 tell you that most people are 'fascinated by the physical' – you should explain this in your own words, e.g. 'what it looks like'. Lines 19 to 24 tell you that the writer is interested in getting 'under the skin' of American life – you should explain this in your own words, e.g. 'know the country fully'. One mark for what he wants to find out and one mark for the reason.

6. The sentence contains long lists of verbs (1 mark), which emphasise that Stephen wants to know every/all aspects of how Americans live (1 mark). OR The sentence contains several clauses/parts (1 mark), which emphasise that Stephen wants to know about several time periods of Americans' lives; childhood, mid-life and old age (1 mark).

> *HINT* — This analysis question is asking you about the pattern of the sentence as well as what the sentence means. You gain one mark for identifying something unusual about the structure and one mark for saying why this is effective. Remember that the main things to look out for when asked about sentence structure are unusual pattern and/or unusual length.

TOP EXAM TIP

At this level, you will usually be asked about the 'effectiveness' of the writer's craft, for example, 'How effective is the author's choice of words?' or 'How effective is the structure the author has chosen?' So you have to work out why these words or structures have been chosen. Writers choose words or structures to create an effect – all you have to do is work out what that effect is.

7. *(a)* He did not want to make a film which was false/would pretend to please Americans or be insincere in its praise of Americans (2 marks).

> *HINT* — The line numbers always help you with where to find an answer. Don't ignore them. Question 7. *(a)* asks you about the phrase 'Without the intention of fawning and flattering ...' The word 'without' is the clue that this phrase tells you what he did not want to do. This is a difficult question so you get two full marks for a correct answer explaining the meaning of 'fawning' or 'flattering'.

7. *(b)* He wanted to make a film which would tell the truth about America (2 marks). OR He wanted to make a film that would show how much he adores America's landscapes/scenery/appearance (2 marks). OR He wanted to make a film that would show many different aspects of Americans' lives (2 marks).

TOP EXAM TIP

Always look at the number of marks to help you work out how many points to make or how much to write.

> *HINT* — Question 7. *(b)* asks you about the phrase 'I did want to make an honest film about America, an unashamed love letter to its physical beauty and a film that allowed Americans to reveal themselves in all their variety'. There are three points here – which one did you choose to write about? This is a difficult question so you get two full marks for a correct answer explaining any one of these three points.

8. They make fun of American stupidity (1 mark) AND/OR Americans' love of money (1 mark) AND/OR American's lack of understanding of sarcasm/sense of humour (1 mark). They think Americans are common/tasteless/crude (1 mark)

AND/OR Americans avoid dealing with/making friends with other countries (1 mark).

> **HINT** — Give two reasons here – one mark for each. There are plenty of reasons to choose from in the sentence 'depth of American ignorance, American crassness, American isolationism, American materialism, American lack of irony, American vulgarity'. You must use your own words here – you will gain nothing for quoting directly.

9. The author establishes a tone of disapproval by using emotive words such as 'silly' and/or 'self-deluding' and/or 'small-minded' (1 mark) which are dismissive (1 mark) OR by using exclamation marks (1 mark) to show his strong feelings (1 mark) OR by using repetition (1 mark) to emphasise his disapproval (1 mark).

> **HINT** — Learners in Intermediate 2 English may find the idea of 'tone' difficult. Just think about tone of voice – someone can use a sarcastic tone, an angry tone, a disappointed tone and so on when speaking. In writing, authors establish tone through the words and structures they choose. Here, you gain one mark for quoting or identifying the word or structure and one mark for explaining how these create the tone.

> **TOP EXAM TIP**
> Emotive words are words which create an emotional impact. Emotive words are often used when the writer is trying to persuade the reader, for example, in advertisements or when the writer is trying to create an emotion in the reader, for example, in poetry.

10. 'Cosmopolitan' means knowledgeable about the world/not limited to one part of the world/not provincial (1 mark) and the phrase 'knowing what the capital of Kazakhstan is' helps me to work this out as it means having knowledge of another part of the world (1 mark).

> **HINT** — The context – that is, the words and phrases which surround a specific word or phrase – usually helps you to work out the meaning of a phrase you may not know. Highlight similar words or phrases or ideas, which may give you a clue to what a word or phrase means. Here, the explanation of what 'cosmopolitan' means appears in the next sentence.

> **TOP EXAM TIP**
> Use a highlighter to highlight key words and phrases in the passage and in the questions.

11. 'offended' (1 mark) AND 'dare' (1 mark).

> **HINT** — Did you spot that the author is describing how the British feel about Americans who do not know very much about Britain? Take care with the last part of the sentence – there are no marks for quoting 'indifferent' as this word refers to Americans and not Britons!

12. This phrase is a metaphor (1 mark) meaning that we do not share the same beliefs/have a different view of life/Americans are not aware of Britain (1 mark).

> **HINT** — The phrase 'not on the map' has a literal and a metaphorical meaning (there is a clue in the sentence as the author uses the word 'literally'). At this level, you should be able to explain metaphors clearly, giving both the literal meaning and the figurative or metaphorical meaning. In other words, explain the comparison that is being made.

13. The word 'so' signals to the reader that the writer is summarising (1 mark) what the writer has explained in the previous paragraphs (1 mark).

> **HINT** — You may be asked about the function of a sentence, phrase, word or idea. Here you are asked about a word. The function of a word means what it does. As you have already read the whole passage, you know that this paragraph is a summary of the writer's arguments and that 'so' tells you this.

14. The author has persuaded me to watch the TV programme as I think it will be different from other films about America – it will be 'honest' (1 mark) and will go into more depth than other documentaries (1 mark).

HINT
You could either quote from the passage or explain your reasons in your own words for full marks here. There are two marks so make sure you explain how successful he has been and give at least one reason.

PRACTICE PAPER B   CRITICAL ESSAY WORKED ANSWERS

EXAM ANSWER ADVICE

In theory, you have 45 minutes to write each critical essay. In practice, however, you have somewhat less time, since you have first to:

(a) select the two questions which you feel you are competent to answer.

(b) reflect on the full implications of the wording of the question by underlining what you see as key words.

(c) plan your material to fit the wording of the question.

Do not allow yourself to be panicked into writing the essay right away; a little time spent on these three stages will result in a much more convincing answer.

In reflecting on the question and planning your answer, remember that the wording of the question comes in two blocks, with the second part usually inviting you to perform two tasks, e.g. *Describe the relationship up to this point ... then show the effect this change ...* It is critically important to balance out your answer over these two parts. Do not spend most of your time on the first part and then discover you have two minutes to consider the second part.

Section A – Drama

EXAM ANSWER ADVICE

The text box before the list of drama questions is a handy reminder of the technical terms that help form an appropriate critical response.

Remember, too, that a play is a theatrical experience and your response needs to take in not only the content of the text, but also the overall effect of this text on the audience as we watch the characters' progress. *As we watch we feel that ...*

1.

HINT
Make sure you choose a play where 'opposing values' are just that: there needs to be a clear distinction between what each character respects. Outline the characters and their values early in your answer.

There is no shortage of plays where opposing values are illustrated through the attitudes and behaviour of characters. Think of Frank and Rita in *Educating Rita* who hold opposing views on the desirability of change; Banquo and Macbeth in *Macbeth* who are divided on the issue of loyalty to their king; or Abigail and John in *The Crucible,* whose personal moralities differ greatly. Consider also the opportunities offered by more minor characters: Reverend Parris and Reverend Hale, for example, in *The Crucible.*

TOP EXAM TIP

Do not drop a quotation into the text and expect readers to know what you are getting at. Lead into the quotation! Give a brief context! *Duncan has a great generosity of nature. Witnessing a badly-wounded messenger collapse in front of him, he demands that he be taken care of:*

'Go get him surgeons.'

2.

State clearly, very early on, the character and the play selected. If a realisation is to be made, you will need to outline how the character viewed himself/herself or the situation previously, as well as how the character reacts to this change.

You will need to think very carefully about your choice of play here. This realisation could be made during moments of reflection, as in a soliloquy, or overhearing the conversation of others, or when a significant revelation is made on stage or as a result of encountering other people. A Shakespeare soliloquy could be the focus here, or the discovery could be the result of a plot mechanism in a modern play such as *Blood Brothers*. Think, too, of the realisation Rita has seeing her mother crying in the pub in *Educating Rita*.

3. To be successful, your answer will need to draw heavily on the various techniques of characterisation and staging which the playwright has employed to bring alive the theme in dramatic (i.e. theatrical) terms. It is not enough to discuss the theme in the abstract.

Section B – Prose

EXAM ANSWER ADVICE

All exam questions need careful study, but questions in this section need more study than most. Prose works come in several forms in this exam: short story, novel, fiction, non-fiction. Be careful not to muddle your genres; if a question is limited to a novel, do not attempt to write about a short story. A question mentioning 'a prose work' is the only one which allows you to examine any of these prose genres. Check carefully before selecting.

The text box reminds you of some of the technical terms which, if used appropriately throughout the text, will make your essay sound academically persuasive to examiners.

A short story allows you room for micro-analysis, but in writing about a novel, ensure that you catch the broad sweep of the text by discussing character, conflict, themes, setting, narrative stance, etc.

4.

'Sustains your interest' invites you to examine perhaps not just the various techniques the author used to characterise this person, but also how he/she may play a part in illustrating a central theme.

Consider carefully the techniques available to an author in creating character: speech patterns, appearance, actions, etc. While your character is 'unattractive' this does not rule out him/her being able to fascinate us by his/her lack of obvious appeal. Make sure you demonstrate *how* this fascination operates on us. Ensure also that you examine how our interest in this character may be sustained by his/her illustrating some aspect of a theme of the text. Is he or she perhaps the opposite in various ways of another, more attractive, character?

5.

Before attempting this question, list carefully the various techniques available to a writer to create 'atmosphere'.

In *Cal*, for instance, the blood and offal of the slaughterhouse act as a dramatic symbol for the mayhem of Northern Ireland during the troubles. Cal's uneasy reaction to the atmosphere in this place also prepares us for his attitude to the troubles in general throughout the novel. In other prose works you may wish to consider the season, the time of day, the weather, the wealth/poverty of the scenes and their effectiveness in preparing us for how we are to view forthcoming events.

> **TOP EXAM TIP**
>
> The introduction to your essay will need to contain a *very brief* summary of the outline of the text in question to place your answer in context. This is the part (the *only* part!) of your essay which you can prepare in advance. It will save you valuable time thinking about how best to summarise your text in the exam room. A good idea might be to link the final sentence of this to the wording of the question.

6. Here you will need to be able to point to a variety of techniques which helped bring alive the society/culture you are referring to. This is not simply a question of describing the surface appearance of people and places (although that is important) but also of analysing how their way of dealing with issues highlights social values. In *The Strange Case of Dr Jekyll and Mr Hyde*, for instance, Utterson and Enfield's roundabout way of discussing matters affecting an important social figure illustrates the hypocrisy of Victorian society, reluctant to confront directly uncomfortable issues.

Section C – Poetry

> **EXAM ANSWER ADVICE**
>
> The text box above the questions is a handy reminder of the terms which will find favour with examiners when used appropriately in your answer.
>
> In those cases where poems you have studied are relatively short, it is a good idea to memorise them. This will provide you with a readily accessible source of evidence for whatever technique you may wish to call on to answer the question.
>
> While detailed reference to the text may be acceptable as evidence in a longer prose work or play, in a poem it is vital to be able to conjure up exact quotations. It is difficult, after all, to discuss onomatopoeia without actually illustrating the sounds in question.

7. Here you will need to get to grips with an experience/event in some detail. Generalisations will not work here. Pinpoint the exact wording that conveys the child's vision and explain the techniques the poet employed to realise this experience/event. Give as many examples as is possible in the time available to you. Also give some thought to how best to deal with the second part of the question inviting you to discuss the poetic techniques by saying 'what effect they have on your response to the poem'. Try to work in phrases such as *The use of onomatopoeia in the line* '*******' *makes me feel* … 'Hamnavoe Market' or 'Mid-Term Break' are just two poems which view life through a child's eyes.

8. This question, like question **7**, requires detailed knowledge of the text and unless you can refer in detail to the text in question, this question is not for you. A similar grasp of how the techniques work on you is also necessary for a successful answer. Read in full the advice for question **7**. It is all equally applicable here.

9.

> *HINT* To answer this question convincingly, you will need to be very familiar with the technical features of a sonnet or ballad you have studied. But it is not enough to spot the existence of quatrain, couplet, octave, sestet, etc. in the sonnet; or rhyme schemes, repetition, etc. in the ballad; you will need to comment on their *contribution* to the overall effect.

What, for instance, is the content of each quatrain in the English sonnet; or the content of the octave and sestet in the Italian sonnet. How does each section reflect a different aspect of the poet's thought? How does this *structuring* of the material work on you? In a ballad, how do the recurring features (repetition, use of numbers, etc.) work on your response to the material?

In other words, how do the *forms and techniques* of sonnet or ballad affect your enjoyment? What does this particular form add to the shaping of the material that any other approach to the material might not?

Section D – Film and TV Drama

EXAM ANSWER ADVICE

There is a good deal of overlap in the language used to discuss film and TV drama, and the language used for prose, poetry and plays. Such features as characterisation, themes, plot and narrative stance all have to be dealt with. But added to these are the subject-specific features listed in the text box above the questions. No serious answer can fail to use an appropriate selection of these terms.

10. In questions of this kind, the listed techniques in the text box above the questions are an invaluable prompt to planning your essay. Ensure that you check out all of them, underlining which particular ones will serve best your answer. Make sure that when you embark on your answer, you place your chosen character clearly in the context of the film/TV drama in question. Is he/she the hero or a key secondary character? Does his/her presentation differ from that of the other characters?

11. Before you begin to deal with the change, make sure you outline the scene/sequence in detail. Once you have done this, carefully explain what your previous response to this person/situation was, maybe suggesting how this response was arrived at before tackling the change. Which techniques achieved this alteration? Were they the same as formed your earlier notion of the situation/character? Again, the checklist in the text box will be very useful in formulating your answer.

TOP EXAM TIP

When discussing a film or TV drama, impress the examiner by acknowledging the director as well as the title of the work in question. If you are hoping to discuss techniques such as music or dialogue, research the name of the composer and writer. You will add authority to your analysis if you can show there is researched background knowledge to your response.

12. In recent years there has been a spate of films that employ the techniques and markers of specific genres, but transform them in various ways, usually for humorous effect. Be sure to outline the traditional techniques of the genre before you turn to how they are transformed or undermined by the director's fresh examination of them. Make use of discussing the presentation of key incidents/scenes or a particular character rather than attempting to cover *all* the transforming features.

Section E – Language

EXAM ANSWER ADVICE

These questions are best tackled only if you have used a Language text in class or you have made a detailed study of various language varieties with your teacher. You must be prepared to analyse language in some detail, citing specific examples at work and interpreting their significance using the technical language indicated in the text box above the questions.

PRACTICE PAPER C   CLOSE READING WORKED ANSWERS

Note: alternative answers are shown by the symbol /. Where the alternative answer is longer, it may also be shown after the word OR.

1. 'mundane' (1 mark) AND 'routine' (1 mark).

HINT
'Mundane' and 'routine' mean 'normal' or 'ordinary'. Always remember to focus on the correct part of the passage. Questions work through the passage in order to make the answers easier to find. So you know that the first question is likely to ask you about the very beginning of the passage. Here you are told to look at the opening sentence.

TOP EXAM TIP

Always pay attention to the line numbers and any advice you are given about where to find the answer.

2. Parents do not make a conscious choice/deliberately choose/are reacting naturally/without thinking/automatically/are used to television (1 mark).

AND

Most Americans do the same thing/it is accepted behaviour in America (1 mark).

HINT
This understanding question is asking you to explain a phrase which has two parts. You gain one mark for explaining the first part ('not so much a parenting decision') correctly and in your own words and one mark for explaining the second part about America ('a national reflex') correctly and in your own words.

3. The writer thinks the tag-line may be an exaggeration (1 mark) as she suggests that the company 'touts' or boasts about its tag-line (1 mark).

HINT
Here, you must work out the attitude of the writer towards the tag-line; in other words, how the writer feels about the tag-line or the company. Attitude is conveyed through word choice. One mark is for identifying her attitude and one mark is for quoting 'touts'.

4. Consumers trust Scholastic/associate Scholastic with educational products/Scholastic is known for its educational products (1 mark) AND 'trustworthy' (1 mark).

HINT
The writer describes Scholastic as 'a company whose reputation is synonymous with education'. Here, you gain one mark for explaining the idea that Scholastic is trusted or known. You gain a second mark for quoting 'trustworthy' from paragraph one.

5. They are described as/claimed to teach children (1 mark) AND they are endorsed/advertised by experts (1 mark) AND these are the products which are available/on sale (1 mark).

HINT
You are being asked to explain: 'The packaging explains why such features are educational, and parents are sure that they read or saw something that an expert said about them. In any case, most people buy these products because that's what is on the market.' There are three different points here. Use a highlighter to pick out the points. Remember, you cannot use any words from the sentence itself such as 'educational'.

6. (a) The writer uses 'wobbly' OR 'lurching' OR 'irresistible' (1 mark) to suggest that the child is cute/very young/vulnerable/unsteady to make the reader sympathise with the child (1 mark).

OR

The writer uses 'irresistible' AND 'monster' (1 mark) to suggest that the child is badly behaved but lovable (1 mark).

6. (b) The writer uses 'frazzled' OR 'defeated' (1 mark) to suggest that the mother is tired/worn out/harassed/has lost control/cannot cope (1 mark).

OR

The writer uses 'happy' OR 'smile' AND 'defeated' (1 mark) to suggest that the mother has lost control but is pleased/glad about this (1 mark).

> **HINT**
>
> Four marks are available here – two marks for word choice related to the child and two marks for word choice related to the mother. So you should quote correctly for one mark and explain what this word choice conveys for the second mark. Two highlighters might be useful here – one to pick out descriptions of the child, and a different colour for descriptions of the mother 'enter the **wobbly** tot, **lurching** around the house as a **frazzled** mother follows with a roll of paper towels and a **happy defeated smile** for her **irresistible** little **monster**'.

7. Children would not understand the advertising/the message of the advertising (1 mark) AND it was considered wrong/immoral (1 mark).

> **HINT**
>
> You should explain the ideas of 'too young to grasp' and 'unethical' in your own words to gain two full marks.

8. The word 'But' signals that the writer is about to/will now explain (1 mark) what has changed/this change (1 mark).

> **HINT**
>
> Remember that function questions are about the purpose of a word, expression or sentence. You should know that the function of a sentence is usually either to link (for example, to link two ideas or two paragraphs) or to signal (for example, to signal a new idea or a further explanation). Here you gain one mark for identifying the function of the word 'but' is to show a change and one mark for knowing that the remainder of the paragraph will explain the change.

> **TOP EXAM TIP**
>
> You should know the meanings and functions of simple conjunctions such as *but*, *so*, *yet*, *for*, and more complex examples such as *whereas* and *nevertheless*.

9. The metaphor 'manned by a battalion' is an army/military term (1 mark), which suggests advertising firms are aggressive/forceful/powerful/well organised (1 mark).

> **HINT**
>
> Did you spot the metaphor? You should be very familiar with imagery such as metaphor, simile and personification. You should also practise explaining images – in other words, working out whether the image is a good comparison and therefore whether it is effective or not. Here you should answer that manned by battalions is a military phrase for one mark, and then explain what this tells you about how these firms operate for the second mark.

> **TOP EXAM TIP**
>
> When you are asked about the effectiveness of a writer's technique, you can explain that you do NOT think it is effective. You must always be able to justify your answer, though.

10. 'Learn' is in inverted commas because the writer thinks the opposite (1 mark) as she thinks that very young children are not learning/does not believe that children are learning (1 mark).

OR

'Learn' is in inverted commas because the writer is using the word ironically (1 mark) to mean that children are not learning (1 mark).

> **HINT**
>
> Writers use inverted commas for a number of reasons:
> - to indicate direct speech
> - at the beginning and end of a quotation
> - to indicate a title or name
> - to indicate a different or unusual meaning of a word or phrase (often used to express irony).
>
> Make sure you know these.

11. The writer describes marketing studies (1 mark) which show that children can recognise products at 18 months (1 mark) OR use names for products at 24 months (1 mark).

OR

The writer describes a study (1 mark) which shows brands are as influential on two-year-olds as they used to be on five-year-olds/children ask for brands before they are three/children are aware of brands at two or earlier (1 mark).

OR

The writer gives examples (1 mark) of brands children recognise, such as Coke (1 mark)

> **HINT**
>
> You should read carefully here. The writer gives three pieces of evidence – the two studies and the examples of product names. You should identify one of these for one mark and explain it for the second mark.

12. It is an example of marketing/advertising language (1 mark) and it achieves its impact because it is short/direct/snappy/catchy (1 mark).

OR

It has an impact because the contrasting/opposite words 'older' and 'younger' (1 mark) are placed next to each other (1 mark).

> **HINT**
>
> Here, you are being asked to analyse the language used – you could comment on tone, structure or word choice. You are asked to explain fully so you need to do more than simply identify an aspect of the language. You must explain why this has an impact on the reader for full marks.

> **TOP EXAM TIP**
>
> It is helpful to know about the different styles of language used for different genres. Marketing/advertising language is an example. Make yourself familiar with the language, tone and structure of non-fiction genres, such as reports, discursive writing, historical accounts.

13. Parents might be interested as 'experts' (1 mark) were speaking at the conference about brain development (1 mark).

OR

Presenters at the conference 'emphasised' (1 mark) that brain development is at its fastest in the first three years (1 mark).

> **HINT** This question is not just about understanding what was said at the conference about brain development. You should consider what you think the effect on parents might have been. Remember, you are also asked to quote to gain full marks.

14. The writer is very persuasive (1 mark) as she uses many examples of research and studies as evidence for her ideas (1 mark).

OR

The writer persuades me (1 mark) because she includes facts and statistics about marketing and companies as evidence for her ideas (1 mark).

OR

The writer is persuasive (1 mark) because she uses emotive language to convince me of her opinions (1 mark).

> **HINT** As always with evaluation questions, you are being asked to make a judgement. So think about whether the writer has persuaded you about her ideas and why you have been persuaded.

> **TOP EXAM TIP**
>
> In answers to evaluation questions, use phrases like 'I think' or 'in my opinion' or 'me/my'. Evaluation questions are about what you think or feel about a passage. You are being asked to make a judgement, so make sure you give your honest opinions.

PRACTICE PAPER C   CRITICAL ESSAY WORKED ANSWERS

EXAM ANSWER ADVICE

In theory, you have 45 minutes to write each critical essay. In practice, however, you have somewhat less time since you have first to:

(a) select the two questions which you feel you are competent to answer.

(b) reflect on the full implications of the wording of the question by underlining what you see as key words.

(c) plan your material to fit the wording of the question.

Do not allow yourself to be panicked into writing the essay right away; a little time spent on these three stages will result in a much more convincing answer.

In reflecting on the question and planning your answer, remember that the wording of the question comes in two blocks, with the second part usually inviting you to perform two tasks, e.g. *Describe the relationship up to this point ... then show the effect this change ...* It is critically important to balance out your answer over these two parts. Do not spend most of your time on the first part and then discover you have two minutes to consider the second part.

Section A – Drama

EXAM ANSWER ADVICE

The text box before the list of drama questions is a handy reminder of the technical terms that help form an appropriate critical response.

Remember, too, that a play is a theatrical experience and your response needs to take in not only the content of the text, but also the overall effect of this text on the audience as we watch the characters' progress. *As we watch we feel that ...*

1.

> **HINT**
> 'Disappointments and setbacks' may come in several forms. The disappointment or setback may stem from a change in a relationship, an upset in a career path or a hope that is dashed in some way. Check your play has a character that will give you sufficient scope to give an interesting analysis of how his/her fate is 'affected in the rest of the play'.

> **TOP EXAM TIP**
> In plays where the title is the same as the name of the principal character, do not irritate the examiner by being careless in your use of inverted commas. Othello is a man; 'Othello' is a play. This is a small point but it is one that says a lot about you and your respect (or lack of it) for academic good manners!

Be careful that in a question of this kind you do not find yourself simply re-telling the plot of the play; give sufficient detail to ensure the context of the disappointment or setback is made clear, but then concentrate on analysing the outcome of this disappointment or setback. This will probably take the form of examining changes in your characters' behaviour, mindset or interaction with others.

2.

> **HINT**
> Start by making clear which theme you have in mind. You may wish to outline briefly the ways in which the theme appears elsewhere in the play. Say, too, why you have chosen this particular scene for analysis, in other words, what is its significance? If you do not know the exact scene number, indicate what the situation is. *This is the scene in which ... It begins when ... The end comes when ....* There is not too much detail here, but it is sufficient to allow the examiner to place your answer.

Keep in mind that a play is more than a text: it is a full theatrical experience; so your answer will benefit from bringing in references to stage directions, the setting and the movements of the characters themselves as well as discussion of the dialogue. For instance, think of the Banquet Scene in *Macbeth*; the stage is an orderly one at the scene's opening, but a shambles at its end. Here what is made graphically clear for us is the theme that the killing of a lawful king brings chaos at many levels. Such an act will always end in total disorder, no matter how hard a usurper may try to pretend all is well.

3. Remember that this relationship may be between family members, say, a husband and wife, parents and children, siblings or members of a community. Remember, too, that 'under strain' does not necessarily suggest an ultimate breakdown, although that *may* sometimes result. Hence the importance of the phrase 'how it was resolved'; be sure to leave time to explore this aspect of the question. Your field of choice here is a broad one, from *Blood Brothers* to *Midsummer Night's Dream*, from *Macbeth* to *The Crucible*. (This latter play is particularly rich in all kinds of relationships that come under strain.)

Section B – Prose

> **EXAM ANSWER ADVICE**
>
> All exam questions need careful study, but questions in this section need more study than most. Prose works come in several forms in this exam: short story, novel, fiction, non-fiction. Be careful not to muddle your genres; if a question is limited to a novel, do not attempt to write about a short story. A question mentioning 'a prose work' is the only one which allows you to examine any of these prose genres. Check carefully before selecting.
>
> The text box reminds you of some of the technical terms which, if used appropriately throughout the text, will make your essay sound academically persuasive to examiners.
>
> A short story allows you room for micro-analysis, but in writing about a novel, ensure that you catch the broad sweep of the text by discussing character, conflict, themes, setting, narrative stance, etc.

4.

> *HINT* A convincing answer to this question will require you to demonstrate a thorough knowledge of the character as the author first presents him/her. Can you refer to an incident or interview early on which establishes this character for you?

You should thereafter be able to refer to specific moments when your view develops through further action or interaction. Is the change in your view brought about by circumstances beyond the character's control, the action of others or a personal decision of some kind? Conclude by summing up in what ways your opinion has changed and by what means this development has been achieved. *The Lighthouse*, *Hieroglyphics* and *All that Glisters* are just three short stories where your sympathy for a character may be seen to grow. Consider also *Its Colours They Are Fine*.

5. This question allows you the broadest of choices. You can write about any text that has caught your imagination with a topic or issue you may not have thought much about before. Be careful, however, not to let your interest in this unfamiliar topic run away with you, to the extent that you end up telling the examiner simply what the text was all about. Your task is to *analyse* how this topic was made interesting or instructive, through the writer's approach to the topic.

6.

> *HINT* Be sure to establish quickly and briefly your initial view of the character before introducing the incident under discussion and the means by which the writer establishes this view. Select your incident carefully and describe it before beginning your analysis of it.

Short stories such as *Mossy*, *The Lighthouse* and *A Deep Hole* surprise the reader with the unexpected. Remember to keep the focus on how this incident was important for your 'better understanding' of the character. In what way were you surprised? Had there been any hint at all of the unexpected development? In what way did your understanding develop? Conclude by saying how your final view differed from your initial one.

Section C – Poetry

EXAM ANSWER ADVICE

The text box above the questions is a handy reminder of the terms which will find favour with examiners when used appropriately in your answer.

In those cases where poems you have studied are relatively short, it is a good idea to memorise them. This will provide you with a readily accessible source of evidence for whatever technique you may wish to call on to answer the question.

While detailed reference to the text may be acceptable as evidence in a longer prose work or play, in a poem it is vital to be able to conjure up exact quotations. It is difficult, after all, to discuss onomatopoeia without actually illustrating the sounds in question.

7.

'A topic affecting family members or society in general' allows you an enormous scope of choice. From Norman McCaig's 'Assisi' to Edwin Morgan's 'Glasgow 5th March 1971' for comment on society; from Liz Lochhead's 'Poem for my sister' to Seamus Heaney's 'Mid-term Break' for topics affecting the family. This is a question where the text box at the head of the section will be more than usually helpful.

8.

You will need to be prepared to discuss in detail many of the poetic devices the poet draws on to illuminate his ideas. Be alert to any shifts in mood on the poet's part. Seamus Heaney's 'Death of a Naturalist' or Edwin Morgan's 'Strawberries' would be interesting choices here. As in question **7**, this is a question where the text box at the head of the section will be most helpful.

9. Identify the event, then go on to discuss how the poet set about creating the atmosphere in the poem. Happiness or unhappiness can be conveyed in many ways in a poem, but perhaps it might be a sensible idea here to pay particular attention to the rhythm selected by the poet, noting if there are any significant changes in it. If there are changes of pace what do they suggest about the dynamic of the mood? Edwin Morgan's 'Trio', George Mackay Brown's 'Hamnavoe Market', Alan Riach's 'The Blues' or Norman McCaig's 'Visiting Hour' might be useful starting points.

Section D – Film and TV Drama

10. There is no shortage of films dealing with modern warfare: *Jarhead*, *Pearl Harbour* and *Saving Private Ryan* are just three films which provide an insightful comment on warfare. Be sure to identify the techniques which betray the director's viewpoint. Recent TV crime drama is similarly rich in examples of series and serials which deal with violence in society. Again, seek out the techniques which reveal the director's view on violence.

11. Once you have chosen your character or theme, examine the text box carefully for hints to jog your memory about how exactly the character or theme was clarified in this scene or sequence. Music? Close-ups? Camera angle? If discussing a character, remember that although your focus is on a single character, his/her character may be depicted in a scene or sequence where there is interaction with others.

12. A character's past is a common area for investigation by filmmakers, keen to throw more light on the personality of the present-day character. Superhero films are often worth examining in this context, but *The Tourist*, *A Single Man* or *The Go-Between* would be interesting choices also. Obviously, flashbacks will be one important technique to consider, but be sure to expand your analysis beyond this.

Section E – Language

EXAM ANSWER ADVICE

These questions are best tackled only if you have used a Language text in class or if you have made a detailed study of various language varieties with your teacher. You must be prepared to analyse language in some detail, citing specific examples at work and interpreting their significance using the technical language indicated in the text box above the questions.

PRACTICE PAPER D   **CLOSE READING WORKED ANSWERS**

Note: alternative answers are shown by the symbol /. Where the alternative answer is longer, it may also be shown after the word OR.

1. The book will contain the writer's memories (1 mark) as an 'archive' OR as a 'storeroom', where historical documents/records/data are kept (1 mark).

OR

The book will be about what the museum is really like/the secrets of the museum (1 mark) because the writer tells us it will 'explain what goes on behind the polished doors' at the museum (1 mark).

> **HINT** You are looking closely at the sentence 'This book is my own storeroom, a personal archive, designed to explain what goes on behind the polished doors in the Natural History Museum.' You will gain one mark for explaining what the book will contain and one mark for a quote which justifies the first part of your answer. You will gain no marks for suggesting that the book will contain facts – this is because the writer tells us it is *his* storeroom and a *personal* archive. So it is written from his point of view.

2. The writer uses imagery/a metaphor in 'tucked away on shelves' OR 'buried deep in the psyche' (1 mark).

AND

This is effective because it emphasises the idea that recollections or facts are secret/hidden/concealed (1 mark).

> **HINT** You have two metaphors to choose from here. Which one did you choose? One mark is gained for identifying the metaphor and one mark for explaining why it is effective.

3. 'I believe profoundly' (1 mark) AND 'I would go as far as to say' (1 mark).

> **HINT** Both these expressions show strong feeling. Note that the phrase 'you can judge a society by the quality of its museums' does not show strong feelings, so you would not gain a mark if you quoted this phrase. Using a highlighter is helpful for picking out words or expressions in both the question and the passage.

4. 'Lustre' could be used to describe some of the precious/shining objects in a museum (1 mark) AND it is used here metaphorically to mean the museum is special (1 mark).

> **HINT** One mark here for explaining that many objects in a museum might be shiny or polished. You gain a second mark for explaining that 'lustre' is used here metaphorically, to mean special, beautiful or splendid.

TOP EXAM TIP

Always read the question carefully. The question will tell you where to find the answer by giving you line numbers and/or quoting the words or phrases or sentences you are to look at.

5. They study/investigate (1 mark) to find out more about the museum's exhibits (1 mark).

> **HINT** 'contributing research' and 'applying learning and scholarship' are the phrases you should explain in your own words. You could use 'study' or 'enquire' or 'search for information'.

TOP EXAM TIP

Understanding questions will often ask you to explain in your own words and you should practise doing this. Simply read an article from a quality newspaper or magazine and pick out words and phrases. Can you think of other ways of saying these words and phrases? Use a thesaurus to help you with this if you find it difficult.

6. 'Pleasing' (1 mark) OR 'warmth … contrasts with the pale stucco' (1 mark) OR 'blue tiles break up the solidity of the façade' (1 mark).

> **HINT**
> You are looking in lines 17 to 20 for descriptions or adjectives which are positive and are associated with beauty such as 'pleasing'. You can choose a single word or a phrase here. Note that you need two examples.

7. Both paragraphs describe the building as a cathedral (1 mark), so this sentence is a link because this paragraph will continue to describe the building as a cathedral (1 mark).

OR

The previous paragraph describes the exterior of the building (1 mark) so the sentence links to this paragraph, which is about the interior (1 mark).

> **HINT**
> Remember that function questions are about the purpose of a word, expression or sentence. You should know that the function of a sentence is usually either to link (for example, to link two ideas or two paragraphs) or to signal (for example, to signal a new idea or a further explanation). Here you are told the function is to link – a link is a connection between two ideas or pieces of information, so you gain one mark for each (for example, one mark for the previous paragraph being about the exterior and one mark for the following paragraph being about the interior).

> **TOP EXAM TIP**
> A sentence may contain a word or phrase that refers back to a previous idea or forward to a new idea. This is what is called 'linking'. Writers sometimes use 'linking words' which make this easier to spot.

8. Visitors are concentrating on/they are looking at/they prefer to look at the dinosaur skeleton (1 mark)

AND

as it is 'enormous'/it gives a 'grinning welcome'/it has 'splendour'/it is in the 'centre' (1 mark).

> **HINT**
> For one mark, explain in your own words that visitors' 'attention is captured' by the dinosaur and not the ceiling paintings. For the second mark, quote the reason for this. Remember to quote to gain full marks.

9. He is pleased/happy to see it (1 mark) OR he is comforted/by it (1 mark)

AND

as it is always the same/it never changes/it stays the same while other things change (1 mark).

> **HINT**
> When you are asked about the writer's attitude, you should look for words and phrases which tell you, the reader, how the writer feels about the topic. Expressions such as 'always glad' and 'consoling' help you here. 'Mutable' means constantly changing. No marks for answering that the dinosaur is like an old friend – the writer clearly writes that he does NOT regard it as an old friend. Take care!

> **TOP EXAM TIP**
> If you are not sure what a word means try to work it out from the context – what does the rest of the sentence tell you which might help you? Of course, Intermediate 2 English will be a lot easier for you if you know the meaning of the words as soon as you read them. Practise for this by reading a quality newspaper or magazine and keep a dictionary beside you. Look up words and phrases you do not know and learn them.

10. People took bones from the tail/bones had to be replaced/staff had to replace bones frequently (1 mark) AND research showed that the *Diplodocus* tail would have been raised to make the animal stable/to make the neck and tail weights equal (1 mark).

HINT No marks here for using 'steal' or 'balance' in your answer as these are used by the writer. Look carefully through the paragraph with your highlighter to find the two reasons here.

11. 'Kids' is an example of informal/colloquial language/slang (1 mark)

AND

the majority of the passage is written in a formal tone (1 mark).

HINT Take care here. There are two marks so you must make two points. Did you spot that 'kids' is one of the very few examples of informal language in the whole passage?

12. The two functions were to display items/objects for visitors to look at/study (1 mark)

AND

to enjoy themselves/amuse themselves/to be entertained (1 mark).

HINT In this question, you are asked to explain 'to examine evidence, as well as to be diverted'. One mark is for explaining 'examine evidence' in your own words and one mark is for explaining 'to be diverted' in your own words.

13. The phrase within the two dashes adds further detail/description of the objects (2 marks).

HINT Dashes are used for many reasons. The most common are to introduce or separate lists or 'extra' information. Here the phrase 'unadorned but for labels' adds more information about the objects.

14. This is very appropriate as this phrase is usually used about animals and where they live/their environment (1 mark).

AND

The phrase is in a passage about natural history/animals in a museum (1 mark).

HINT In this answer you should explain that 'natural habitat' is usually used to refer to animals. It is being used here to refer to a person, which is unusual. You could answer that the phrase is appropriate or not appropriate, but always justify your answer by explaining fully (as the question asks you to do).

15. The writer's main purpose is to inform as he includes facts and statistics about the museum (1 mark), such as that it is like a cathedral and that it contains public galleries that 'take up much less than half of the space of the Natural History Museum' (1 mark).

OR

The writer's main purpose is to persuade readers to visit the museum (1 mark) as he uses phrases such as 'I believe profoundly' (1 mark) OR he describes its beauty/size/interesting exhibits (1 mark) OR he explains that he will 'reveal' information about the museum and the people who work there (1 mark).

HINT This question asks for your opinion so it is acceptable to answer that you think the purpose is to inform or to persuade. Just remember to include clear justification for your answer by explaining your choice.

PRACTICE PAPER D — CRITICAL ESSAY WORKED ANSWERS

EXAM ANSWER ADVICE

In theory, you have 45 minutes to write each critical essay. In practice, however, you have somewhat less time since you have first to:

(a) select the two questions which you feel you are competent to answer.

(b) reflect on the full implications of the wording of the question by underlining what you see as key words.

(c) plan your material to fit the wording of the question.

Do not allow yourself to be panicked into writing the essay right away; a little time spent on these three stages will result in a much more convincing answer.

In reflecting on the question and planning your answer, remember that the wording of the question comes in two blocks, with the second part usually inviting you to perform two tasks, e.g. *Describe the relationship up to this point ... then show the effect this change ...* It is critically important to balance out your answer over these two parts. Do not spend most of your time on the first part and then discover you have two minutes to consider the second part.

Section A – Drama

EXAM ANSWER ADVICE

The text box before the list of drama questions is a handy reminder of the technical terms that help form an appropriate critical response.

Remember, too, that a play is a theatrical experience and your response needs to take in not only the content of the text, but the overall effect of this text on the audience as we watch the characters' progress. *As we watch we feel that ...*

1. Be careful that your answer does not turn out to be too one-sided. Yes, spend sufficient time discussing why you find the outcome for this person 'deserved' and give plenty of reasoned evidence for your opinion, but remember that it is unusual for a playwright to introduce a 'good' character without flaws or a 'bad' one without merit. Be sure not to overlook a brief discussion of this. The phrase 'handling of this character' could suggest not simply personal characterisation, but also his/her treatment of another character or behaviour in a relationship.

TOP EXAM TIP

Take care with questions where the second part gives you a choice of responses to write about. If you see an '**or**' in the second part, be sure to stick to your choice and not drift between the two. If you do, you will end up answering neither part in a fully focused way.

2. There is a breadth of opportunity here, which allows you to write about a great many plays. Keep in mind that, depending on your choice, there may be a double aspect to the 'workings' of this 'concern': its effect on the person in the grip of this mindset and its effect on others with whom he/she interacts. An exploration of both would give you a convincing analysis. Do not forget to give *your* response to the relevant character(s) as you watch the outcome taking shape.

3.

> **HINT**
>
> This is a question where re-visiting the text box above the drama questions would, as usual, be useful, but consider, too, elements such as contrast with previous scenes or movement between characters on the stage (i.e. towards or away from each other) or who is significantly present or absent.

A scene becomes 'memorable' by a variety of theatrical devices, so be careful not to limit your response to an analysis of the text alone. Do not overlook the phrase 'the reasons for its appeal to you'; make sure you offer your personal response to this scene and why you find it 'memorable'.

Section B – Prose

> **EXAM ANSWER ADVICE**
>
> All exam questions need careful study, but questions in this section need more study than most. Prose works come in several forms in this exam: short story, novel, fiction, non-fiction. Be careful not to muddle your genres; if a question is limited to a novel, do not attempt to write about a short story. A question mentioning 'a prose work' is the only one which allows you to examine any of these prose genres. Check carefully before selecting.
>
> The text box reminds you of some of the technical terms which, if used appropriately throughout the text, will make your essay sound academically persuasive to examiners.
>
> A short story allows you room for micro-analysis, but in writing about a novel, ensure that you catch the broad sweep of the text by discussing character, conflict, themes, setting, narrative stance, etc.

4.

> **HINT**
>
> Criticisms often manifest themselves in presenting us with sympathetic characters in emotive situations, but carefully chosen symbols and settings (seasons and weather as well as places, remember!) are often useful ways, too, for writers to underline what they want us to think and feel.

The choice of text you select here is broad: the short stories of Anne Donovan in her collection *Hieroglyphics* offer some quite sharp present-day observations on the treatment of children and old people; *The Cone Gatherers* and *The Strange Case of Dr Jekyll and Mr Hyde* in their very different ways offer criticisms of society in previous times.

5.

> **HINT**
>
> This could be a question that leads you simply into re-telling what happens in the course of the text. That is not what the question asks. *How* the author helped you 'understand it more fully' is the focus. In a fiction text, the 'issue' may be revealed through treatment of character or setting or outcomes; in non-fiction, your understanding may be aided by comment from several sources, anecdotes, statistics, comparisons, etc. Be alert to the *means* whereby your understanding was helped.

In a question like this, the field of fiction and non-fiction choice is an extensive one: *To Kill a Mocking Bird* is an obvious choice for a novel dealing with racial intolerance, as is the more recent *Small Island* by Andrea Levy. Consider also the texts already mentioned in this section for fiction encompassing novels and short stories for the other issues.

> **TOP EXAM TIP**
>
> Successful critical essays require evidence. This can be either detailed reference to the text (in your own words) or quotations from the text (in the author's words) if you are writing about a play or a prose work. If you are writing about a poem, evidence should usually take the form of a quotation.

6. Alan Spence's *Its Colours They Are Fine* is a collection of fascinating tales which grip the imagination, yet the 'action' is slight in many cases. *Tinsel* would be one well worth analysing to discover why we are so moved by the story's end. Anne Donovan is another short-story writer, where our imagination is caught without any showy action in many of the short stories in her *Hieroglyphics* collection. For 'means' refresh your memory by checking out the text box above the prose questions.

Section C – Poetry

> **EXAM ANSWER ADVICE**
>
> The text box above the questions is a handy reminder of the terms which will find favour with examiners when used appropriately in your answer.
>
> In those cases where poems you have studied are relatively short, it is a good idea to memorise them. This will provide you with a readily accessible source of evidence for whatever technique you may wish to call on to answer the question.
>
> While detailed reference to the text may be acceptable as evidence in a longer prose work or play, in a poem it is vital to be able to conjure up exact quotations. It is difficult, after all, to discuss onomatopoeia without actually illustrating the sounds in question.

7.

> **HINT**
>
> This is a question which, more than most perhaps, demands a strongly personal response from you. It is not enough to discuss the techniques where the subject or setting or speaker is conjured up by the poet (although this is, of course, necessary). You need to make clear to the examiner why there was a strong appeal to you as well.

Many of the poems you may have studied for this course could be useful here, some under *either* subject *or* setting *or* speaker: 'Porphyria's Lover' or 'In Mrs Tilscher's Class' are just two that might produce excellent answers under any one of the three headings. 'Valentine', 'Death of a Naturalist', 'Visiting Hour', 'Brooklyn Cop', 'Aunt Julie', 'Glasgow 5th March 1971' might reward investigation under one of the three headings.

8. Both modern and traditional poetry are rich in examples written in Scots. From the ballad tradition onwards, excellent poems in Scots have delighted readers. Poets from Robert Burns and Walter Scott, through to Liz Lochhead and Duncan Glen, have exploited the richness of the vocabulary, sounds and rhythms of the Scots language. Liz Lochhead's poem 'Bairnsang' even juxtaposes the same content in both Scots and English side by side, making the characteristics of Scots even clearer when set beside its English version. Be careful to emphasise what it is in *the use of Scots itself* that 'affected your enjoyment'.

9. Here you might wish to look back to the ballad tradition, poems like 'The Twa Corbies' or 'The Wife of Usher's Well', where the story line is always strong. Later traditions could give you poems such as 'Glasgow 5th March 1971' and 'Child with Pillar Box and Bin Bags', where there is narrative at the heart of the poem. Remember, however, to put sufficient emphasis on *how* the poet managed to 'engage your interest' in the story. Beware of merely re-telling the story itself; pay plenty of attention to the techniques employed to 'engage your interest' in the story.

Section D – Film and TV Drama

EXAM ANSWER ADVICE

There is a good deal of overlap in the language used to discuss film and TV drama and the language used for prose, poetry and plays. Such features as characterisation, themes, plot and narrative stance all have to be dealt with. But added to these are the subject-specific features listed in the text box above the questions. No serious answer can fail to use an appropriate selection of these terms.

10. The field is rich here, with humour being employed to make serious points, from the social comment in films such as *Hairspray* and *Groundhog Day* to the political satire of *Primary Colors*. TV series such as *The Simpsons* and *The Office* also use humour, often to make serious points. Make it clear always, however, how this humour 'affected your understanding' in terms of characters and themes. Use specific examples to underpin individual points.

11.

HINT — Television may suggest more immediate possibilities than films, but take time to consider also the many films made in Scotland. Once you focus on them, they may offer more scope for comment than some of the more obvious TV offerings.

With problems in the oil industry, *Local Hero* is enjoying a new vogue; *Rob Roy* and *Braveheart*, from a much earlier historical era, present a view of Scotland which is rich in possibilities for comment; don't overlook either *Gregory's Girl*, *The Prime of Miss Jean Brodie*, *I Know Where I'm Going* or *Laxdale Hall*. TV series such as *Taggart* or *Rebus* are also useful fields for study. Remember that this 'view' of Scotland will be created by more than a story line: choice of settings, music, characterisations, camera work all need to be taken into consideration.

12. This question offers a wide scope, since there are very few films or TV series you may have studied that do not include a character who is unfortunate in some way. It invites you to concentrate on the 'means' used by the director 'to enlist your sympathy for the character'. This requires you to consider not only characterisation (physical/mental/personality/language traits) but also his/her social context (relationships, integration into community, etc). Is the fact that this character is 'unfortunate' a result of personal shortcomings or due to forces

outside his/her control? When examining the *means* whereby you feel yourself drawn to this person, remember your answer will need to consider items such as setting, music and camera angles, in addition to characterisation and social positioning.

Section E – Language

EXAM ANSWER ADVICE

These questions are best tackled only if you have used a Language text in class or you have made a detailed study of various language varieties with your teacher. You must be prepared to analyse language in some detail, citing specific examples at work and interpreting their significance using the technical language indicated in the text box above the questions.